IT'S REALLY VERY SIMPLE

Jack McArdle ss cc

It's Really
Very Simple
UNCOMPLICATING THE MESSAGE

the columba press

This edition, 1994, published by
the columba press
93 The Rise, Mount Merrion, Blackrock, Co Dublin, Ireland

First edition 1985
Cover by Bill Bolger
origination by The Columba Press
Printed in Ireland by Genprint Ltd, Dublin

ISBN 1 85607 093 X

Contents

Introduction

I was coming out of a church one evening after preaching a sermon on something or other, when a little old lady caught me by the arm and whispered in a sincere and confiding way, 'God bless you, father. I'm going to pray for you, because even I know what you're talking about.'

I wrote this book with that lady's words in mind. I wrote it in the hope that she, and anyone reading it or hearing the ideas expressed, would know what I was talking about.

In presenting these ideas and insights in book form, I hope to provide a source of help to many people. Preachers and teachers may find it helpful to have basic Christian truths presented in unclouded language. The many illustrations and anecdotes may prove helpful in preparing homilies or religion classes. People in Christian leadership roles (Prayer groups, etc.) may find here a simple pulling together of basic gospel messages and essential Christian truths. Even my little old lady may pick up this book. If she does, she may begin anywhere she wishes, read any chapter of her choice, and still know what I'm talking about!

As well as the preachers and teachers, I also am concerned about the searcher. It is my hope that the stark basic presentation of some of the truths in this book may provide the necessary break-through for someone who is searching, and encourage that person to go on then to read and study books of greater substance.

This book is offered with love, and with a prayer that you may be blessed in the reading of it as I have been blessed in the writing.

Jack McArdle ss cc
Summer 1985

The gospel is simple

When Jesus's disciples returned to report to him how following his instructions had brought such wonderful results, he was filled with the joy of the Holy Spirit and said, 'I praise you, Father, Lord of heaven and earth, for hiding these things from the intellectuals and the worldly wise, and for revealing them to those who are trusting as little children. Yes, thank you, Father, for that is the way you wanted it' (Lk 10:21). Jesus received arguments from the lawyers and hugs from the children. His feet were washed with the tears of a sinner and an outcast, while the Pharisees complained that his disciples hadn't washed their hands.

The gospel is so very simple, that it is amazing how we succeed in complicating it! Kierkegaard, the philosopher, once said to Hegel, another philosopher, 'We philosophers are extraordinary geniuses. We can take the simplest concepts, and by the time we're finished with them, we will have put them into lang-uage that very few can understand. Last week I was in Copenhagen where I met another philosopher, and when I asked him for directions to a street not very far away, he gave me a map of Europe.'

The gospel can be summarised in one sentence: God loves me, and in one word: *Abba* (daddy). Everything Jesus did or said was an invitation to come under the Niagara of the Father's love, and let him love me. In Matthew's gospel, chapter 6, he says: 'Remember, your Father knows exactly what you need even before you ask him. When you pray, say 'Our Father ... give us this day our daily bread.' So don't worry about having enough food and clothing. Your heavenly Father already knows perfectly well that you need them and he will give them to you if you give him first place in your life, and live as he wants you to.'

For this message to be heeded, it must be heard by those who are in need. Not much point in speaking about forgiveness to someone who believes he is perfect! Only the hungry will express a real interest in the word 'food'. How often have we heard the person who has eaten a big meal say 'Don't mention the word 'food' for the rest of today!' Jesus came to bring forgiveness, food, and freedom to those who acknowledge their need for this. There will be little response to a word like Abba (daddy) from someone who has lost the heart of a child.

There is a simplicity about children, a directness,

an uncomplicated approach, that cuts right through our best-thought-out theories. This simplicity is completely unrelated to ignorance or stupidity, and can be illustrated by the story of the film *Whistle down the wind*. A group of children find a tramp in a barn, whom they believe to be Jesus. When their kitten gets sick, they bring it to 'Jesus', and when the kitten dies, they have many questions to ask: 'Why did Jesus let the kitten die? Why do people die? What is this whole business of death?' They run to the nearest Church in search of answers. They are ushered in to the priest, who is having his tea. Their opening question is direct: 'Why does Jesus let people die?' The priest responds with an answer which is pious, proper, and correct. He uses theological words, precise words, 'God' words, as he formulates an orthodox answer. Then he pours himself another cup of tea and seems quite satisfied. As the children walk away, one little boy turns to his older sister and says, 'He doesn't know either, does he?'

For those who are hungry, who are weak, who feel burdened with guilt, whose boat is tossed and battered on the sea of life; for those who feel lost, who are afraid, who are alone; to such people the gospel must be simple, and it must speak to them. The gospel must be seen, not as a message to a world, but to a person here, to another there, on a very personal level. From the personal dimension will come the communitarian and social dimension.

One rainy Saturday afternoon a father found himself looking after his children at home, while his wife went shopping. To keep his ten-year-old son busy, he tore a map of the world out of an old magazine, cut it into several pieces, and invited his son to re-assemble it as a jigsaw puzzle. To the father's amazement the boy presented him with the completed puzzle within a few minutes. 'How did you do it so quickly, son?' he asked. 'It was easy,' the boy replied, 'I didn't know what the world should look like, and I just couldn't make any sense out of all the lines and dots. Then I noticed part of a man's face on the back of one of the pieces, so I turned them all over, put the man together, and the world was OK!'

Another beautiful example of a child's ability to cut through to the heart of the matter is contained in a story about a three-year-old child strolling through a cemetery with her dad. She looked at the graves and the head-stones, and asked, 'Daddy, what are those?' The father fumbled a reply, 'Eh, these were people who lived in those houses down there. Then one day, holy God sent for them to come and live in his house with all his angels.' 'And Daddy, did they go off to live with holy God, in his house?' 'Yes,' said the father, unsure what the next question would be. The little girl's face lit up with a flash of understanding, and, as she looked up into her dad's face, she said, 'And Daddy, do you know what? When they went off to live in holy God's house, I bet you this is where they left their clothes!' Yes, indeed, even profound mysteries can be revealed to little children.

Not all children are simple, even if they do retain their directness. 'Where did I come from?' the young son asked his father, while in the course of writing an essay. 'Santa Claus brought you,' said the father, who did not believe that all questions really have to be answered! 'And where did you come from?' 'Oh, the stork brought me,' was the father's throw-away answer. 'And grand-dad, where did he come from?' The father held his ground firmly and replied, 'He was found under a head of cabbage.' The young lad returned to his writing and, after a while, he closed the copy and went upstairs to bed. The father was puzzled by the suddenness and persistence of the questions, so he checked the boy's copy, where he read, 'After persistent questioning, it is my firm conclusion that there has not been a normal birth in this family for three generations!'

Isn't it time we told the children the truth, especially if the questions have to do with the truths of the gospel?

God loves me

I believe that, when I die, and come face to face with Jesus, he will ask, 'Did you come to really believe that my Father loved you? I don't care how long it took you, but did you finally get the message? To speak that message was the reason I came.' Jesus came to put this simple truth beyond all question or doubt.

One of my own haunting mental images of Jesus is to see him praying to the Father on the mountainside at night. I see the tears streaming down his face as he repeats over and over again, 'Father, they don't believe me. They don't believe me. I told them about the prodigal son, and the forgiving father, just as you told me, but they still are burdened with guilt, and are afraid to come home to you. I told them about the birds of the air, and the lilies of the field but they still fret and worry over many things. Father, they just don't believe me.' 'The world's sin is unbelief in me,' he said at the Last Supper (Jn 16:9).

The saint is not the person who loves God, but the person who is completely convinced that God loves him or her. To know that God loves me is to look at my life and see the evidence for myself. It is not enough to believe it just because someone told me. I should be able to look back and be amazed at how I 'came through that', 'overcame this', 'survived the other'. I know a young woman who came through a great tragedy some years ago, in which most of her family was wiped out. Her courage at the time was extraordinary, and today she can jokingly admit that she would be up on a chair screaming if she saw a mouse! She had heroic courage when it was needed. That's what's called our 'daily bread', just what's needed at a particular time. When I begin to see this pattern in my life, I become convinced that my Father is looking after me.

On his thirteenth birthday, a young Indian brave was placed in the middle of the jungle and told to spend the night there, as a test of nerve and bravery, before being accepted into young manhood in the tribe. It was a long, long night. Every leaf that fell, every branch that creaked, every creature that moved in the undergrowth, caused a shiver of fear to pass through him. He never knew a night could be so long; there was no hope of sleep, and, more than once, he was on the verge of running away. Finally, after what seemed like ages, the dawn began to filter through the trees, and slowly his vision adjusted to the growing light. As he peered around, he was really surprised to see his father standing behind the nearest tree, gun in hand. He had been on guard there all night! The boy's first thoughts were, 'If I had known that my father was standing on guard like that, I would have slept soundly all night!' When I die, and express any surprise at how my Father had watched over me in life, Jesus could surely say, 'But I told you that! That was the very reason I came. The night of life need not have been so anxious after all!'

God's love is not a conditional love, in so far as he loves me anyhow, and, because he is God, he can-not but love me. God *is* love and he can only love 100%, and never less, whether I am in his grace or not. God never stops loving me, but I can prevent his love reaching me, or limit its influence and effect on me. From my point of view there is noth-ing automatic about God's love, or indeed, about the message of the gospel. Jesus came 'for the fall as well as for the resurrection of many.' (Lk 2:34-35). The onus is on me. 'Your heavenly Father will give you what you need, if you give him first place in your life, and live as he wants you to' (Mt 6:33). The offer and the promise never change, but they are fruitless if not accepted and acted on. There are two parts to salvation history, what Jesus did, and what I do about it. The man of medical science can come up with the cure for your complaint, but nothing happens until you take the medicine!

Jesus over-looked Jerusalem and cried. He wanted to do so much for them, but they wouldn't let him. 'Eternal peace was within your reach, and you turned it down', he wept, 'and now it is too late' (Lk 19:24). Jesus didn't want Judas to hang himself, but he certainly wouldn't stop him. He offers me peace, his peace, but I am free to live in misery and die of ulcers, if I chose to! The gospel is an invitation with RSVP clearly marked on it. The offer, the invitation, is always present. The result is determined by my response.

Let me put it this way. Suppose I'm sitting here under a spotlight. I'm dazzled, and everything around me is clear and bright. If I go outside and close the door behind me, the spotlight still continues to shine, but I have put myself beyond its light. It's not the light's fault if it is not shining on me.

Let me put it another way. There has just been a shower of rain. I go out and examine the ground. One part of the ground is quite dry, another part has a pool of water on it. The same amount of rain fell on all areas. Some spots allowed the water soak through, while other areas were crusted and hard, and the water could not penetrate. 'God allows his rain to fall on the just and unjust as well' (Mt 5:45).

I repeat the truth that God loves me. There is a story of a young priest who delighted his new congregation with his first sermon after arriving in the parish. The following Sunday, people came from far and near to hear him, and he preached the exact same sermon. He repeated his sermon the third Sunday. This brought one concerned person to the sacristy after Mass to diplomatically point out what was happening, and to enquire if he had any other sermon, and when it might be expected. 'Oh, I have several other sermons,' the priest assured his visitor, 'and I will be delighted to move on to the second as soon as I see you doing something about the first one!' If I fail to grasp and accept the basic truth of the Father's great love for me, then there's no point in going on to consider anything else in the gospel.

John's gospel is very profound theology, the conflict between life and death, light and darkness, good and evil, Jesus and Satan. Many years later, as an old man on the island of Patmos, he had reduced the whole message to one basic concept: 'God showed how much he loved us by sending his only Son into this wicked world to bring us to eternal life through his death. In this act we see what real love is: it is not our love for God but his love for us when he sent his Son' (Jn 4:9-10).

In his prayer at the Last Supper, Jesus prayed that 'they may know, Father, that you love them as much as you love me' (Jn 17:23); and again, 'so that the mighty love you have for me may be in them' (Jn 17:26). Jesus prays that we may know the Father's love and he surely expects us to pray for this also. He also says, 'No one knows the Father except the Son, and he to whom the Son chooses to reveal him' (Lk 10:22). To pray, 'Jesus, reveal the Father to me' is a beautiful and a very necessary prayer.

Jesus Christ

Pride was the original sin. The creatures wanted to become as exalted and as powerful as the creator, the clay wanted to take over the place and role of the potter. From their lowly state, made of clay and close to the earth, the fact that Adam and Eve even presumed to raise themselves to the level of an almighty sovereign God, was also a grave sin of foolishness and presumption. But God is also a God of love and extraordinary forgiveness. Instead of wiping them off the face of the earth into total annihilation, not only did he forgive them, but he devised a plan, in his unbounded love, that would raise mankind to the level of the divine, and make it possible for him to share in the life of the divinity. 'For God so loved the world that he sent his only Son' (Jn 3:16). Jesus came into the jungle of life to carve a way for us that would lead us back to the Father. 'I am the way,' he told his disciples, 'No one can come to the Father except through me' (Jn 14:6).

In the early Church, the followers of Jesus were known as followers of the way, because Jesus was seen clearly in that capacity. 'He who follows me does not walk in darkness, but has the light of life' (Jn 12:46). It is not an easy way, because there is no easy way, and there is no other way. Jesus did not choose the easy way and he asks us to follow him. 'If you want to be my disciples, you must take up your cross daily and follow me' (Lk 9:23). It is a sure way, a certain way, and it is *his* way. Jesus leads, I follow.

In my brokenness and sinfulness, I won't always be walking step by step with him. Did you ever notice a mother walking along a footpath with a small child? One moment they are walking hand in hand. Next moment, she pauses and calls on the child to come on, as he looks in a shop window, or becomes distracted by something lying on the footpath. Yet another time, he is running on ahead of her, and she is calling on him to wait for her, as there are dangers up ahead, intersections, open manholes, etc. and, of course, he will probably get tired, and she may have to carry him for a while. This, in practice, reflects our journey with Jesus. Like the mother, he keeps us close to him, and we too will arrive home at journey's end.

It is important that we know who Jesus is. 'Who do you say that I am?' he asks (Mt 16:15). Jesus tells us clearly who he is. He is all of God, the Son of God. 'He who sees me sees the Father,' he assured Philip

(Jn 14:9). 'I and the Father are one' (Jn 10:30). There is no hidden agenda, no undisclosed message. 'If you had known who I am, then you would have known who my Father is. From now on you know him and have seen him' (Jn 14:7). Jesus goes to great pains to assure us that there is nothing hidden, that his message is a complete one, that the Father has nothing to add. In simple language, Jesus tells us that he came to tell us all about the Father, and later on, 'The Holy Spirit, the source of all truth, he will come to you from the Father, and will tell you all about me' (Jn 15:26).

Jesus is all mankind, the Son of Man. We, humans, share a common nature, we are all part of that entity known as humanity, humanhood, and sometimes called mankind. Whatever it has to offer, that's what we get. If it is damaged and prone to evil, then that is what we will experience ourselves to be. If it is purified, made new, raised to a new level, then that change, that newness, belongs to me as well. Jesus took on all of sinful, broken, disobedient humanity, and by living a perfect life (as a man) without sin, and in total obedience to the Father, he rescued and redeemed humanity, and made it possible for the state of original sin and blemish to be totally reversed. There is nothing automatic about this, of course. There are two parts to this whole story, what Jesus did, and what I do about it. I could hold out a book towards you until I get a pain in my arm, but it does not become yours until you come and take it.

I remember, years ago, when the rural electrification came to our part of the country. The poles were sunk in the ground, the wires were put up, and most people said 'yes', and had their houses wired and connected. There were some who said 'no', however, and, to this day, the electric wires still pass by their front door, while they read by the light of an oil lamp.

Jesus is all God and all of mankind, the Son of God and the Son of Man. He is the meeting place of God and man, the person through whom alienation is healed and reconciliation effected. He is the vertical beam (God to man) and the horizontal beam (man to man). He gave himself so totally in obedience to that mission that he died on the cross, the union of the vertical and the horizontal.

It was Christmas Eve, and a man was discussing with his wife how odd it seemed that God should have chosen to come on earth as a helpless babe. It certainly would not be his idea of drawing much attention, or of making any great impression. As he spoke, his attention was drawn to some sort of commotion going on outside in the garden. He looked out, and saw five green geese, floundering around in the snow. They obviously had become detached from a migrating flock that had passed by. Anxious to help in some way, he ran into the garden, and his appearance created total panic among the frightened geese, as they flapped their wings, and continued to sink in the soft snow. He opened the garage door and tried to direct them in, in the hope of getting some conservationist group to come and collect them. The more he tried to help, the more frightened they became, and they were in great danger of injuring themselves. For one desperate moment, he wished he were a goose, and, in their own language, he could tell them that he was concerned about them, and was only trying to help them. We are not told what happened to the geese, but the man himself saw clearly right there why Jesus came the way he did. By becoming one of us, he could speak our language, tell us clearly what he was about, how he could rescue us, and that we could trust him, and not be afraid.

That central question comes up again and again: 'And you, who do you say that I am?' (Mt 16:15). If I can accept the fact and face the reality of my own brokenness, sinfulness and limitedness, then I may be open to seeing Jesus as my saviour, because I am ready to admit that I need one. If I am prepared to clear away the worries, pre-occupations and ambitions from the centre of my life, and to put Jesus there, then I am saying he is Lord, and I am making him Lord of my life. If, because of Jesus in my life, there is nothing impossible, then I have accepted him as God.

Jesus is a very personal God, and he asks very personal questions: 'Who do you say that I am?' (Mt 16:15). 'Will you also go away?' (Jn 6:67). 'Do you love me?' (Jn 15:2). I must never presume he is in the crowd, at the prayer meeting etc., unless I meet him, see him, hear him, speak to him there. Mary and Joseph made that mistake one time. They 'assumed he was with his friends, among the other travellers' (Lk 2:44) on their way back to Jerusalem, and they had to spend three anxious days searching for him before they found him.

Before I come to know Jesus, I have to meet him. I meet him in prayer. Prayer is giving him time and space in my life; it is working on my relationship with him. It is essential that I come to know Jesus, and not just know *about* him. 'I am the Good Shepherd; I know mine, and mine know me' (Jn 10:14). If you hear me speak about someone, you will easily know whether my information is hearsay, or from a book, or whether I speak from personal acquaintance and with first-hand knowledge. A group of men once sat around discussing good and bad memories. As a result, a bet was placed about which of them could recite Psalm 23

('The Lord is my Shepherd') by heart. The first man had a clear pleasant voice, and some training in the art of dramatics. He began, 'The Lord is my Shepherd, there is nothing I shall want.' His recitation was flawless and was greeted with loud applause. He even had to recite it a second time, to greater applause. The second man was very old, rather stooped, with a crackling voice that required an effort to be heard. He began, 'The Lord is my Shepherd, there is nothing I shall want,' and when he was finished, there was total silence all around the room. Then, one by one, each man present lowered his head and began to pray quietly. The first man to recite the psalm stood up and explained the great difference in the response to both recitals of the same psalm. He put it very simply: 'I know the psalm,' he said, 'but that old man – well, he knows the Shepherd.' It is just not enough to know the psalm.

Jesus is very firm and definite in his demands about following him and taking him seriously. There is not one 'maybe' or 'might' in the whole gospel! 'He that is not with me is against me, and he that does not gather, scatters' (Mt 12:30). There is a story about an impetuous young man who saw a beautiful woman walking through a park, and immediately began to follow her. The woman, aware of being followed, turned and asked why he was following her. 'Because,' he said, 'you are so beautiful, and I am so much in love with you. I love you more than anyone who ever walked this earth.' She replied, 'If you look behind you, you will see my younger sister coming, and she's much prettier that I am.' The young man turned quickly, but there was no one there. 'You are mocking,' he said, 'there's no one coming behind me.' 'If you were so much in love with me, why did you turn around?' was her retort, as she walked away.

The reason why Jesus is so insistent on his way, is that he knows there is no other way! He loves us too much, and he paid too high a price to be half-hearted in his invitation, or indecisive in his demands. He knows he is the answer, an answer to all of our questions. As with the rich young man (Mt 10) Jesus laid down the conditions, and was sad when the young man walked away. But Jesus would not change the conditions, or modify his demands. Jesus does not change. 'He is the same yesterday, today, and always' (Heb 13:8).

His kingdom

Chapter 12 of Revelations is a necessary backdrop to understanding the kingdom that Jesus came to establish. In that chapter we read about Satan being defeated by Michael the Archangel, and being forced from heaven. Four times in that account we are told that Satan 'and all his armies were cast down to earth.' That is why, when Jesus came, he referred to Satan as 'the prince of this world' (Jn 16:11). To look around the world, even today, and to see its struggles and to see its values, is to have ample proof that Satan is, indeed, the prince of this world.

The kingdom of the world has its own values. Your God can be power, wealth, influence, politics or fame. People are relatively important, depending on their usefulness, social status, or authority. Your power comes from your political clout, your bank account, or your ability to make yourself heard and heeded. The kingdom that Jesus came to establish makes very little sense against such a background, and to one with the mind-set of the world.

No wonder they put a crown of thorns on him and laughed. That is still the attitude of the world.

Pilate asked Jesus: 'Are you a king then?' and he replied, 'That is why I came' (Jn 18:32). 'I am not an earthly king. If I were, my followers would have fought ... but my kingdom is not of this world' (Jn 18:36). The kingdom Jesus came to establish is diametrically opposed to the kingdom of this world. In his kingdom he is Lord, everybody is important, and we live by the power of his Spirit. This is radically opposed to a kingdom where material values are worshipped, where the unimportant are expendable, and where power comes from the flexed muscle or the clenched fist.

Jesus told us to cheer up, because 'it has pleased your Father to give you the kingdom' (Lk 12:32), and he tells us to pray 'Thy kingdom come' (Mt 6:10). We pray that the kingdom become a reality for us, that we discover it, and that we make the necessary decisions for living in it, and by its rules. It is like 'a pearl of great price, a treasure hidden in a field, which, when a man discovers, he covers it over again; then he goes, sells all he has, and buys that field.' (Mt 13:45). In simple language, Jesus is saying that the kingdom and entering into it, should receive our all. Nothing in our lives must come between us and kingdom-living. Jesus presents us with the same truth in another way: 'Seek ye first the kingdom and its justice, and all other things will be added onto you' (Mt 6:33). In other words, if you give your attention and efforts to the kingdom, I will take care of everything else in your life. This is a central promise in the gospels. There is a condition here, and if I meet that condition, then I have a sure and certain promise that God will take care of everything else.

The kingdom of the world is based on prudence, caution, reason and intellect, and it makes sense up in the head. It is a controlling manipulative kingdom, in which people are pawns, and passing glory is the prize. The kingdom of God is based on love, service, sharing, and giving, and it appeals to the heart. The key to the secrets of this kingdom is prayer. To come aside, to be alone with Jesus, to give him time and space, to listen to him – that's when he teaches me the secrets of the kingdom. When he was alone with his disciples, away from the crowds, he told them, 'To you is given to understand the mysteries of the kingdom, but to the rest in parables' (Lk 8:10), and again, 'You are permitted to know some truths about the kingdom that are hidden from the others' (Mk 4:11). Unless I give him time and space in prayer, I cannot expect to grasp his message of the kingdom. Listening is at the heart of prayer, and prayer is not us talking to God who doesn't hear, but it is God speaking to us who won't listen! Listening to him speak, then responding to him, that is the proper order in the dialogue that we call prayer. If I don't listen to him, if I don't hear him speak, then I am responding to nothing; in other words I'm speaking to myself! 'The Pharisee stood up, and prayed thus to himself' (Lk 18:11).

In the movie *The Ruling Class*, a man in a psychiatric hospital thinks he's God. When the psychiatrist asked him when he first discovered he was God, he replied, 'I was praying and praying for years and years, then one day I woke up and discovered I was only talking to myself!'

The road to heaven *is* heaven and we call that the kingdom. I get nothing when I die that I'm not offered now. The only difference when I die is that I will he able to see and understand it, and, having the proof, I won't need faith anymore. Today I have a father, a mother, a Saviour; his peace, joy, abundant life, and his Spirit. What else is there, except to be out of this body, and to have the freedom to enjoy it all? Just as the road to heaven *is* heaven, so the road to hell *is* hell. Some people think the road to heaven is hell, and that the road to hell is heaven!

Jesus came 'to bring good news to the poor' (Lk 4:18). It is only fitting, then, that the poor should have a special place in his kingdom. 'Blessed are the poor in spirit for theirs is the kingdom of heaven'

(Mt 5:3). It is a kingdom for children, for the lowly, the humble, the poor in spirit. 'Anyone who humbles himself as this little child is the greatest in the kingdom' (Mt 18:4). 'Anyone wanting to be the greatest must be the least, the servant of all.' (Mk 9:35). He took a basin of water and a towel and, as he washed their feet, he showed them what true greatness is. 'Anyone wanting to be a leader among you must be your servant ... your attitude must be like my own, for I, the Messiah, did not come to be served, but to serve'(Mt 20:25-28).

'It is almost impossible for a rich man to get into the kingdom. I say it again, it is easier for a camel to go through the eye of a needle than for a rich man to enter the kingdom' (Mt 19:23-24). It is not a virtue to be poor, but to be poor in spirit, to be detached, to let go of my possessions so that others may benefit. Dives, the rich man (Lk 16:19-31), did not end up in hell because he was rich. Dives had much more than he needed, and there was a poor man (Lazarus) on his doorstep who did not have the necessities, and Divos refused to share. That was his sin, and that is what would make it impossible for him to come into the kingdom. An unwillingness to share, and the tendency to hoard to myself, and for myself, much more than I actually need, is in direct conflict with kingdom living.

Living in the kingdom brings God's guarantee of

my daily bread, just sufficient for now. 'Your heavenly Father knows your needs. He will always give you all you need from day to day, if you make the kingdom your primary concern' (Lk 12:30-31). There is a story about a man who died and found himself in a place where, if he was thirsty, a little lad ran in and gave him a drink of water; if he was hungry another little lad ran in and gave him plenty to eat; if he was tired, a bed was wheeled in for him. Any wish he expressed was immediately granted. After a while he began to get bored with the monotony and predictability of it all. Even things he wanted, but didn't really need, were provided. He called one of the little lads over. 'Can I do without anything here?' 'No,' was the reply. 'But even things I just fancy, but don't really need?' 'You will be given them,' he was told. 'And is this going to go on for all eternity?' 'It is,' was the reply. 'Oh no!' he said, 'I'd be better off in hell!' 'And where do you think you are?' asked the little lad!

Kingdom living has a unique richness of its own. 'The man in the kingdom takes out of his storeroom things old and things new' (Mt 13:52). Pity the person who is locked in the past, who is clinging solely to the old in matters of religion. Equal pity for the person who rejects the old and is in continuous search for the new and the novel. 'To live is to change, and to become perfect is to have changed often,' said Newman. The ideal balance is to retain the riches and wealth of the old, and to enrich it further with the ongoing revelation and enlightenment of the new. I know many from an older generation, while still cherishing the treasures of their devotions, novenas, and pious practices, can still go along with great enthusiasm, bible under arm, to a charismatic prayer meeting. That, to me, is part of the freedom of living in the kingdom.

The kingdom now, becomes heaven later on. Like the thief on the cross beside him, if we ask him to remember us in his kingdom, he offers us paradise today (Lk 23:42-43). It is a narrow gate, and few there are who find it (Lk 13:24). However, Jesus is the way, and following him is a sure and certain guarantee of entering his kingdom now and for eternity.

Invitation

The dimension of invitation is very real in the gospel. Jesus came with an invitation to a feast being offered by the Father. He himself describes his mission thus, in Luke 14:16-24. There is, indeed, a double invitation – they were invited to the feast, and then, when the meal was ready, they were told to come along. Jesus certainly is almost speaking tongue-in-cheek when he describes the excuses that were offered for not coming to the feast. One man had bought some oxen and must try them out – as if anyone would first buy and then examine, or first buy and then try out! Quite obviously, the excuses were not genuine, but the invitations were issued, and they could never say they were not given a choice, or allowed make a decision. The invitation sorts out those who are interested, and those who are not. That will be the stark truth facing us all, good and bad, when we stand before God in judgement – we were invited, and the decision to accept or refuse was ours.

There is another level on which this idea of invitation is seen in the gospels. If I want to meet Jesus, to live with him, to come to know him, I am invited to 'Come and see' (Jn 1:34), to come and see for myself. The shepherds were told about Jesus by angels, and yet they said, 'Let us go to Bethlehem and see for ourselves this wonderful thing the Lord has made known to us' (Lk 2:15). When Nathaniel questioned Jesus' credentials, the other disciples simply said, 'Come and see for yourself' (Jn 1:46). The woman at the well brought out all her friends to meet Jesus, and at the end of it all, they had a very independent response to her: 'Now we believe because we have heard him ourselves, not just because of what you told us' (Jn 4:42).

At the heart of this invitation is the call to a personal experience, to experiential or empirical knowledge. It is a long journey from the head to the heart, from academic to experiential knowledge. I could have a doctorate in theology, and have all the correct theological definitions and answers, and not believe a bit of it in the heart. Being invited to come and see for myself is to ensure that I end up believing, because in my heart, I know I have experienced it – and not just because someone told me.

It is out of this personal experience that the conviction comes. At the beginning of the gospel I am invited to 'Come and see' (Jn 1:39), and at the end I am told, 'Go and tell' (Mk 14:15). If I have come and seen I will want to go and tell. I will speak with a conviction that will be real evangelism and not mere catechesis. A Christian is in the business of attracting, not promoting. If I go into your house and I have chicken-pox but I tell you I have measles, which will you catch – what I have, or what I said I have?

A television programme showed three women in a supermarket with trolleys. They have been given two minutes to fill their trolleys with as much as they could, and the one with the highest value of goods at the check-out would be the winner. The whistle was blown, the women charged down the aisles, bumping into each other, grabbing items from the shelves, and really entering into the spirit of the rat-race they were involved in. Their behaviour was so typical of our world – pushing, jostling, grabbing, the value of a person's work being judged at the cash register. When they arrived at the check-out they were out of breath and quite anxious; and as they looked at other's trolleys, they said, 'Oh, I never saw that item, ' 'I only wish I had taken two of those.' Again so like the world – always something missing, some unfulfilled dreams. Now let me change the story slightly. In this version there is a fourth woman, and she has really come to know Jesus as her personal saviour; from her own experience she knows of the Father's love and care. The whistle is blown and off they go, charging down the aisles. The Christian is looking relaxed and at ease, and seems to be in no hurry at all. She picks up a loaf of bread, which she puts in her trolley. She picks up an item off the floor and says to one of the other women, 'Excuse me, you dropped this.' She then picks up a pound of butter for herself and moves on down to the check-out. The three women arrive there in a state of near collapse, and the fourth is standing there with a smile on her face that thoroughly annoys them. Misery loves company, and if you look saved you'll annoy a lot of people! One of the women looked into the fourth woman's trolley, and with utter scorn, asked, 'Who let you out? Didn't anybody tell you what this whole thing is all about? And why are you smiling anyhow?' The woman remained calm and composed throughout this and whispered to her attacker in a confidential tone, 'Actually my father owns the supermarket!' This surely is a case of no explanation is possible for those who don't know; and for those who know, no explanation is necessary. I cannot really describe or explain an experience to you. I can only hope to invite you to come and share it with me. That's why Jesus stresses his invitational approach.

We often use the word 'practising' when we speak of our religion! What I am speaking of is more a question of experiencing than learning, of being guided and directed more than being taught. It is accepting an invitation to a feast and being nourished at the feast. There can be a vast difference between being religious and being spiritual. Religion can possibly stop at the external practice, without any deep personal involvement. To be spiritual is to experience the message and respond to it at a much deeper level. On the morning of Pentecost, Jerusalem was full of religious people – 'devout men having arrived from every nation' (Acts 2:5) – and yet when they met spiritual (spirit-filled) men, they thought they were drunk! (Acts 2:13). Jesus said, 'Not all who are religious are really godly people. It is not those who say "Lord! Lord!" who will enter heaven' (Mt 7:21) Calling him Lord, if he is not Lord, brings no advantage!

There was a man who loved to go to prayer meetings and tell how he had been touched, and how his life was changed. He always began with a long list of the evils that were in his former life – lying, cheating, stealing, drinking, wife-beating, etc. When he was finished his list, he would smile happily and say, 'I thank God that, throughout all those years of sin, I never lost my religion.' This is what can happen when religion is divorced from spirituality, when the gospel is presented as a set of rules, rather than as an invitation to an experience that leads to conversion.

On the morning of the resurrection there were two

small groups of Jesus' friends on two different roads, not very far from each other. One road led into Jerusalem, and on that road could be seen a group of women highly excited, with obvious good news, and they were on their way to tell his disciples that Jesus was alive, they had met him, and had spoken with him (Mt 28:11). The other road led to Emmaus, and on it were more of Jesus' friends, but they were defeated, dejected, and were obviously without any good news. They had heard a rumour, of course, that he was alive, but they themselves had experienced none of that (Lk 24:13-30). At the end of their journey, however, they experienced the Risen Lord, and, as always happens, they just had to run off to tell someone about it. (Lk 24:34)

What is a Christian?

Jesus came to carve a way for us out of the jungle of life. If we follow him on that way we will get back home to the Father. Following him on that way is to do what he did, to live like he lived. It means feeding hungry people, be-friending the outcast, living in total obedience, and carrying a cross. To follow Jesus on that way is to be a Christian. Christianity is about a person, Jesus Christ. It's about making myself available to him to continue his work on earth. The incarnation is ongoing, in that Jesus wishes to be formed in me also, so that, through me, he can continue to heal a broken world.

In the early Church, there was a central truth that influenced them deeply, and we seem to have lost sight of that over the years, and that was that Jesus had gone away. He went away one time, but he came back three days later. Then he brought them up to the top of the mount of Olives, said good-bye, and he went away. He did not come back, even though they were expecting his return at any moment. Their constant prayer was, 'Maranatha,

Come Lord Jesus!' In one of our own prayers we use the words, 'As we wait in joyful hope for the coming of our Saviour Jesus Christ.' After Pentecost, the apostles had a very simple message, made up of four parts:

1. The Messiah, who was promised, did come and his name was Jesus.

2. He was crucified, but God raised him from the dead.

3. He returned to the Father in glory, where he is now.

4. He will come again at the end of time.

The Jesus they knew was so full of love and kindness that his coming again was also seen as good news.

Yes, Jesus had gone away, but he had a very special plan in which he would send us his Spirit, and we could supply the body – and so we could actually make him present. Since his ascension he has no body on this earth except the one that is formed by his Spirit, when he unites us into a unity, a family, a community, a church. This is what we call the Body of Christ. A Christian is one who is deeply committed as a member of that Body, and who unites himself in love and unity to the other members.

Christianity is about a person, Jesus Christ. It means living in his kingdom, and becoming like him in my dealings with others. 'Who do you say that I am?' is the basic question of Jesus to all Christians. 'Who are you saying that I am by the way you act towards others? Are you saying that I am moody, temperamental, grudging, unforgiving?' As a Christian I show who I think Jesus is by the way I treat others.

Five men arrived by taxi at a railway station just as the train was about to pull out. They jumped from the taxi, dashed across the platform, and boarded the train as it began to move. In their dash across the platform, one man had accidently hit a table with apples on it, and had scattered some of the apples. One of the other men, who was a Christian, and striving to live a Christian life, jumped from the train at the last moment, when he saw the scattered apples, and shouted out to the others, 'I'll catch up with you this evening sometime.' He returned to the platform, where he found an eight year-old boy seated at the table. The boy was blind. He was waiting for his mother to return from a shop across the road. The man picked up the apples, stacked them up neatly, put the damaged ones to one side. Then he handed the boy some money, saying, 'This should take care of the damaged apples. I'm sorry for what happened. I hope we haven't spoiled your day – and God bless you.' As the man walked away, the young blind boy called out after him, 'Sir! Sir!' 'Yes,' said the man, as he turned around. 'Sir, are you – are you Jesus?'

Mahatma Ghandi, as a young immigrant worker in London, was given a copy of the gospels to read, and, when he had read them, he said, 'When I read the gospels, I came to admire your Christ – and to despise your Christianity.' A Christian is someone who lives the gospel. I may be the only gospel some people will ever read – they may never buy the book. How appropriate the verse I read on a card somewhere that went something like this:

You write a new page of the gospel each day
by the things that you do,
the words that you say.
People read what you write,
whether faithless or true.
– What is the gospel according to you?

The ideal of Christianity is to see Christ in everyone, and to be Christ to everyone. Whatever about the possibility of being Christ to everyone, I am not at all sure about the possibility of seeing Christ in everyone. There are some people and I even wonder how God the Father can see Christ in them! There is a secret to this mystery. It the secret of ministry or service. As soon as I begin to really minister to another, the Christ within that person will reveal himself, will become evident. Faith requires that I do the ministering first, because if the revelation came first, there would be no need of faith.

In a world of revolution, in a world of bombs and bullets, the weapon of revolution put into the hands of every Christian is the cross. The cross means putting other people before oneself. The cross was intended for Barabbas, not for Jesus, but Barabbas walked off scot-free while Jesus took his place. St Maximilian Kölbe saw a man being taken off to be executed, so he stepped forward and offered to take his place. He died in that man's place, and while Maximilian was proclaimed a saint in 1983, that man, then 83 years of age, was present with tears streaming down his face. He had actually met a man who could be described as a real Christian.

If Jesus had died in any other way, the cross is still an excellent symbol of a meaningful religion. What comes from God (vertical) must go out to others (horizontal). Unless forgiveness goes out sideways from me to others, it doesn't come from God. If judgement and condemnation go out from me to others, that's what I draw down on myself from God. God doesn't want to hear me tell him, 'I'm sorry, I love you, I thank you, I praise you,' unless the others in my life hear it also. If I want to know the exact and precise depth of my love for Jesus, I have to look sideways and see who is the person in my life that I love least. 'That's exactly how much you love me,' says Jesus. 'Whatever you do to the least of these, that you do unto me'(Mt 25:40).

In so far as a Christian is part of the Body of Christ, is an instrument through which Christ continues his work on earth, is his hands and feet in the doing of that work; in so far as Jesus continues to be incarnated in each of us, to die and to be resurrected in us, – to that extent it can be said that the Christian's real call is to become Christ. There is no higher vocation possible for sinful man.

Sin

Jesus says, 'You are my friends, if you do what I command' (Jn 14:28). To obey Jesus is to love him, and to sin is to love something else instead. 'Do you love me more than these?' Jesus asks Peter, after Peter had denied him (Jn 21:15). Jesus is a clear and definite way back to the Father. To choose any other way is a sin – 'Going my way', 'I did it my way' could be suitable titles for sins, as well as films and songs!

Sin is never an accident, or even an act. It is an attitude, a disease, and the act is just a symptom of that disease. There is a basic rebelliousness within us. We are in a state of sin. I am a sinner by nature. Sin comes naturally to me. My sins are the only things that are really mine – everything in me that is not sin or sinful is through the grace and power of God. 'If we say we have no sin, we are only fooling ourselves, and refusing to accept the truth. If we claim we have not sinned, we are lying and calling God a liar, for he says we have sinned' (1 Jn 1:8-10).

There is a story of a man who picked out six of his friends at random, and sent each a telegram that said simply, 'All is known, leave at once.' Five of them left town immediately! For the average person, who is reasonably normal, the conscience is not too far beneath the surface! I often think of a dog I had when I was a boy; he always looked guilty whenever he did something wrong! One look at him, and I knew he had chased the postman, or taken something off the kitchen table. My conscience, through turning the deaf ear, can become blunt, and lose its edge. I can justify anything after a while, if I work at it. The greatest lies I tell in life are the ones I tell myself. If I could be totally honest with myself, and stop rationalising and justifying behaviour that I know to be wrong, then I could become totally honest with God and with people as well.

We sometimes hear it said that we are living in an age that has lost its sense of sin. Where you have a situation-ethic mentality, where we can make up the rules as we go along, then we can arrive at a stage where anything can be justified. In other words, if I were a 'good' moral theologian, I could reason my way through and out of every situation! But a sin is a sin is a sin. If God wanted a permissive society he would have given us Ten Suggestions, and not Ten Commandments! I remember a funeral in my local town several years ago. Men stood at the corner as the funeral passed by. 'Too bad about poor Mick, he went suddenly enough.' 'Ah indeed. What did he die of, did you hear?' 'I don't rightly know, to tell you the truth, but, as far as I know, I don't think it was anything very serious!'

Sin is serious. It damages, and sometimes can sever my relationship with God. I am punished *by* my sins as well as *for* them. My sins hurt me and harm me, take from my peace, and burden me with guilt. Jesus loves me too much to stand idly by. With his eyes nearly closed on the cross with blood, tears and spittle, he looks upon me and cries out, 'Father, forgive him – he knows not what he does.' I believe that if I knew the harm my sins do me, I could never sin.

In Romans 7, Paul bares his soul with extraordinary openness and honesty. He certainly had no doubt at all that he was a sinner, was in a state of sin. It is well worth letting him speak for himself: 'I don't understand myself at all, for I really want to do right, but I can't. I do what I don't want to – which I hate, and I know perfectly well that what I am doing is wrong, and my bad conscience proves I agree with the laws I am breaking. But I can't help myself, because I'm no longer doing it. It is sin inside me that is stronger than I am that makes me do these evil things' (Rom 7:15-17). I would do a great injustice to Paul, and to truth, if I were to end the quote there, because that is only part of what he says, and it could be interpreted that I am a sinner and there's nothing can be done about it, so I may as well give up, and settle for my state. Paul goes on to ask, 'Who can save me from my slavery to this deadly lower nature? Thank God! It has been done by Jesus Christ our Lord. He has set me free' (v25).

Jesus came to tell us all about the Father, and he then sent the Spirit to tell us all about him (Jn 15:26). Jesus came to set us free, to pay the price for redeeming us, and he then sent his Spirit 'to convict the world of sin' (Jn 16:8). It is the Spirit of God within us that gives us a deep sense of sin. To use a modern word, we are 'conscientised' to injustice and to evil.

Pride and selfishness are at the root of my sinfulness. A frog, living in a forest in New Jersey, persuaded two geese to fly him to Florida for the winter. He tied the ends of a long cord to each the goose, he held the centre of the cord in his mouth, and off they went. The journey was going well until someone on the ground noticed the strange sight passing by overhead. 'Hey, look at that!' he shouted 'that's fantastic. Whose idea was that, I wonder?' In his anxiety to get the credit for being so clever, the proud frog opened his mouth and shouted: 'Mine!' The Fathers of the Church have always said that humility is the mother of all virtues.

There are two vital ingredients for getting to heaven, one is to be a sinner, and the other is to know it! In a Charlie Brown comic strip, Linus comes up to Charlie and says, 'Charlie Brown, do you want to know what's the trouble with you?' Charlie Brown says, 'No.' In the third panel they just stare at each other, and then Linus says, 'The trouble with you, Charlie Brown, is that you don't want to know what is the trouble with you.'

In another cartoon, a man is seen with a very smug expression on his face. His wife is slightly turned away from him, and is praying quietly, 'Dear God, please give Mr Perfect one tiny flaw!'

A basis for holiness is to have a deep awareness of my sinfulness; this ensures a real dependence on God's grace, and the absence of a tendency to judge and condemn my fellow sinners. The saint knows that he cannot be the first to cast a stone at anyone.

Repentance

Jesus lived on this earth for thirty-three years. He spent thirty years preparing and three years presenting a message that his Father sent him to proclaim. I often think that if Jesus had only three minutes in which to present his message that he could have told us the story of the prodigal son, and in it, he would have retained the heart of the spirit of the message. There is the forgiving father, the wayward son, and the self-righteous son who had never left home, and who also badly needed a change of heart. The father would never go to where the son was feeding pigs. The decision to come home, and to face the truth, had to be the son's decision, and his only. This is at the core of repentance. 'The truth will set you free,' Jesus tells us (Jn 8:32). There is a difference in maturity between saying, 'I did wrong', and then showing that it was someone else's fault, and to admit, 'I was wrong', and to accept the truth as it is. Christianity is a way of life for mature adults with children's hearts.

Some years ago I worked in a girls' prison in

America. I remember speaking to a girl who was leaning up against a wall chewing bubble-gum, and when I asked her what she had done that merited her being in a place like this, she told me she had thrown her baby out a thirdstorey window. She was high on drugs. I asked her why she did this, and she said that he wouldn't stop crying. There was no sign of remorse or emotion, and the bubbles from the gum seemed to convey a total sense of bored indifference. The following morning she came swaggering down the corridor, again with the bubble-gum and, of course, the usual foul language as she was passing the other girls. She walked straight into my office, without knocking, and slammed the door shut with her heel. Then suddenly there was a change. It was safe now, the door was closed, and the other girls couldn't see her. The bubble-gum came out of the mouth, was thrown in the basket, and she flopped into a chair and began to cry. She was in bits, afraid, guilty, and home-sick, but she was afraid to let the other girls see her like this. As I watched her, I was conscious of one aspect of God's call to repentance: 'Will the real you please stand up?'

The call of the gospel is a call to come home. Humankind had wandered away from the garden, and the Father sent Jesus to bring us home. Jesus picks up the lost sheep and carries it home on his shoulders. He doesn't drag it along behind, or drive it along in front. The call to repentance must be heard in the heart. It can never be forced. There was a little girl who was misbehaving and really giving her mother a rough time. The mother told her to go and sit in the corner until her father came home. The little girl went over and stood in the corner. She refused to sit, as she continued her rebellion. After another hassle, the mother literally forced the child to sit down. When the father came in, he asked the child what she was doing, and she said, 'Well, on the outside I'm sitting down, but inside I'm still standing!'

The way that Jesus opened up for us is clear and definite. We follow him on that way: we live as he lived. It is a path of obedience, of submission, of formation that leads to transformation. It is not walking on a path that is parallel to his way, because this, in effect, could mean walking independently on the other bank of a river. Repentance means crossing over the bridge that he provides and walking in obedience to him. Repentance is a way of life for the sinner. I cannot give myself to God at any one time. I am like a vast tract of uncultivated land, and Jesus redeems me area by area, bit by bit, piece by piece. Today he is challenging me about my use of time, tomorrow about saying 'thank you' a bit more often, the next day about walking in truth of action and conversation. It is a continual on-going process that must never be let up. There will always be a tension in my life between how I am and how I ought to be. This tension is good. It can be compared to an electric socket in a wall. There is a positive and a negative wire in the socket, and without this there would be no power.

Quite a lot of our sin could well be in the area of omission – the good things we don't do. In Albert Camus' novel, *The Fall*, there is a devastating line that expresses the truth of how narrow our lives can become. There is a scene where a respectable lawyer, walking in the streets of Amsterdam, hears a cry in the night. He realises that a woman has fallen, or been pushed, into the canal, and is crying out for help. Then the thoughts come rushing through his mind. Of course he must help, but … a respected lawyer getting involved in this way? What would the implications be? What about the natural danger? After all, who knows what has been going on? By the time he has thought it through it is too late. He moves on, making all kinds of excuses to justify his failure to act. Camus writes, 'He did not answer the cry for help. That is the man he was.' That is the man he was! What a sad description of a person who sins by doing nothing. As we say in the Confiteor, 'I confess … that I have sinned … through my own fault … in what I have done, and in what I have failed to do.'

For the Christian, repentance is part of everyday

living. Repentance is as necessary for the spiritual life as breathing is for the physical existence. It is part of the on-going conversion, of the daily decision that is needed to walk with Jesus. Because I am a sinner by nature there is a deep-set instinct within me that continually draws me away into the easy option, or the line of least resistance. Paul speaks of the battle or struggle that Christian living entails, 'there is something else deep within me, in my lower nature, that is at war with my mind' (Rom 7:23), and Peter writes about 'the bodily passions, which are always at war against the soul' (1 Pet 2:11). To engage in that battle is to strive continually to walk the path of repentance and obedience .

Satan had come down on this earth (Rev 12) in pride and disobedience. Jesus came from the extreme opposite angle, in humility and obedience. Living as Jesus wants us to live is to have the heart of a child. It is to get out from behind the masks and barriers, and become like little children. Jesus was serious when he told a group of rough uncouth fisherman that he wanted them to become like little children, if they wished to enter his kingdom (Lk 10:15). A child is naturally trusting and finds it comparatively easy to have faith in people. Jesus said that the sin of this world is unbelief in him (Jn 16:9). We do not believe, we do not trust, because we have lost the heart of a child.

The gospel is an invitation to come home, and to allow God love me. The Father sent Jesus to invite us to 'turn around and come back to me with all your heart; don't let fear keep us apart'.

The *New York Post* carried the story of a group of young people travelling by bus, on a holiday trip to Fort Lauderdale in Florida. Not long after leaving they noticed a dark-skinned middle-aged man, poorly dressed, and looking quite worried, as he sat slouched in his seat, head down. When the bus pulled in at a road-side cafe, everyone got out except Vingo, as the young people had named him. The young people were curious about him – where had he come from, where was he going? Finally, one of them sat next to him and said, 'We're going to Florida. Would you like some of my coke?' He took a swig and said, 'Thank you.' After a while he told his story. He had been in a New York prison for four years. 'While I was there, I wrote to my wife and told her that I'd be away for a long time, and if she couldn't take this, she should just forget about me. I told her not to write or nothing. And she didn't. Not for three and a half years.' Then he added, 'She's a wonderful woman, really good, really something.' 'And now you're going home, not knowing what to expect?' the girl asked. 'Yeah,' Vingo replied, 'You see, last week when my parole came through I wrote to her again. I told her I would be coming by bus. As you come into

Jacksonville, where we live, there's a big oak tree. I told her that if she'd take me back, she could tie a yellow ribbon on the tree, and I'd get off the bus and come home. If she didn't want me, forget it; no ribbon, and I'd keep on going.'

The girl told the others and soon they were all involved, looking at pictures of Vingo's wife and children, and all getting more anxious and nervous as they approached Jacksonville. There was a hushed mood in the bus. Vingo's face tightened. Then suddenly all of the young people were up out of their seats, screaming and shouting, crying and dancing. All except Vingo. He just sat there stunned, looking at the oak tree. It was covered with yellow ribbons, twenty or thirty of them! The oak tree had been turned into one big welcome banner. As the young people shouted, Vingo rose from his seat, made his way to the front of the bus, smiled back at his young friends through a flood of tears, and got off.

No wonder a song was written about it, a song about the welcome for the prodigal when he arrives home. It would require very little change to turn this song into a hymn.

Sacrament of Reconciliation

We have sacraments to celebrate the major decisions of our lives, such as the decision to join the Christian community, to come into full communion with that community, to accept personal responsibility in the community, to get married, to be ordained a priest in that community. We also have a sacrament for accepting and receiving the healing power of Jesus. And finally, we have the great sacrament of reconciliation, when we acknowledge that we have strayed from the path we chose in our baptism, and confirmation, and we now want to come home. Most sacraments are a once-and-for-all decision, and can be received only once. Because of our sinful nature, and the basic rebelliousness within us, we need the sacrament of reconciliation frequently.

A sacrament is a decision, and it includes within itself the grace or power to carry out that decision. We call this latter part 'the grace of the sacrament.' I make many, many decisions in life, but, of course, I don't sacramentalise every decision. John and

Mary could decide to live together, or they could come to Church and sacramentalise their decision in the sacrament of matrimony, and receive the grace and power of the sacrament to carry out what is now a sacred decision. A sacrament is a decision that must be lived. In other words, the acid test of a sacrament is what happens when I come out after receiving or celebrating the sacrament. John and Mary get married in Church, but now they have to go and give meaning to that ceremony. The ceremony depends on the future to give it meaning. Sacraments can die, and lose all life. Living sacraments are like arteries in the Body of Christ that bring his blood to the members. The arteries can become blocked and be no longer life-giving. John and Mary could be still under the one roof, and I could be still functioning as a priest, but our sacraments could be dead for years, and no longer life-giving.

I make many many decisions in the area of repentance, but if I am really serious about carrying out those decisions, I will have to sacramentalise many of them. If I need forgiveness for the past, I don't need this sacrament. Does that shock you? My intention is not simply to shock but to challenge you, and to compel you to think. The condition for forgiveness is to have forgiveness in my own heart for others. If I have unforgiveness in my heart towards another person, then I do not receive forgiveness, even if I receive this sacrament. On the other hand, if I have forgiveness in my heart for others, then my sins are forgiven, whether I go to this sacrament or not. I know this requires further explanation, because it is not the total picture.

Forgiveness is a necessary condition for receiving forgiveness, but that is not all. I could have forgiveness in my heart and continue to sin. I must, of course, repent of my sin, ask Jesus to forgive me, and if I meet the condition of forgiving others, then I can know that I am forgiven. I can repent of my sin, ask Jesus to forgive me, meet the condition of forgiveness, and receive forgiveness – and yet not receive the sacrament of reconciliation. That is why I said that if I need forgiveness for the past I don't need this sacrament.

Let me explain this further. Many people seem to go to this sacrament trying to change yesterday, wanting sin to be washed away without trace, as if those things hadn't happened. I cannot change yesterday. It went away at midnight and will never return. 'Lord, give me the serenity to accept the things I cannot change' – and that includes the past. The only value the past has are the lessons it taught me. I would be very wise today if I learned every lesson that life taught me. The wise man is the man who learns the lesson from yesterday, and then makes a decision that will change tomorrow. A sacrament is essentially forward-looking. I acknowledge my sin, of course, and I confess it, and then I make a decision that will ensure that that sin is not repeated. In the sacrament of reconciliation I receive forgiveness for the past, plus the grace of the sacrament to carry out that inherent decision. I then go back out, and do what I can to give meaning to the sacrament by carrying out the decision I have made, knowing that the grace of the sacrament is sufficient for me to do that.

A man returned to his car in the parking lot and found a note under the windshield wiper. It read as follows: 'I have just smashed into the side of your car. The people who saw the accident are still watching me. They think I am writing down my name and address on this piece of paper. They are wrong!' 'Going to confession' as we often describe it, must be so much more than just something I do for a special occasion. The acid test is the attitude of repentance I bring to it, and the sincerity of the resolution I bring away from it. As I said earlier, the real test of my sincerity is how I try to live the sacrament when I go back out.

The sacrament can do so much more than just forgive sins. It is a sacrament of healing in that it can heal the wounds of sin. It is a sacrament of peace, in which I can meet Jesus as my personal saviour and come away knowing that I am forgiven. It is a sacrament that I can *celebrate* in the fullest meaning of that word.

This is a sacrament of salvation – a sacrament of starting again. When I travelled by train as a child, I used to be fascinated as I looked out the window and saw the wire dip, and then rise and disappear from view, as I passed the telegraph poles. It was up and down, lift and dip all the way. My life is like that. It tends to dip, to sag, to slide. In a marriage situation a couple may have a tiff or a few harsh words, and usually an apology will set things right again. The sacrament of reconciliation is more than just an apology to God. If the marriage rift becomes so serious that a third party is called in, the main problem is identified, serious decisions are made, the marriage vows are renewed, and they may throw in a second honeymoon for good measure! That's how seriously I should approach the Lord in this sacrament of reconciliation. I have been unfaithful to my part of the covenant. I must identify the breach, admit my guilt, ask for forgiveness, and the grace to return to fidelity, and begin to walk with the Lord in obedience once again.

This sacrament has had a very 'bad press' in many areas over the years, and many sincere penitents met anything except the love, gentleness and acceptance of Jesus Christ when they approached this sacrament. While I do not defend this in any way, I still must point out that some of the problems people experience as they approach (or don't approach!) this sacrament are due to a lack of appreciation of two basic truths of the gospel. I am a sinner in constant need of forgiveness and salvation, and Jesus is a loving saviour who sits and awaits my return to him. The greatest thanks I can give Jesus for dying for me is to make full use of the results of what he has done. 'We can all be saved … by coming to Christ, no matter what we are, or what we have been like. Yes, all have sinned; all fall short of God's glorious ideal. Yet now God declares us 'not guilty' of offending him if we trust in Jesus Christ, who, in his kindness, freely takes away our sins' (Rom 3:22-24). In a world of bionic women and six-million dollar men, of course, it is becoming more difficult to admit to human weakness, brokenness, and a real inclination towards evil! Some people would prefer to pay hefty fees to their psychoanalysts to help them deal with their guilt, than to return like the prodigal son and admit that 'I have sinned against heaven and against you' (Lk 15:21). I heard a leading psychiatrist state one time that he could discharge many of his patients that very day if he could get them to deal with their guilt.

I leave the final word to the psalmist: 'What happiness for those whose guilt has been forgiven! What joys when sins are washed away! What relief for those who have confessed their sins, and had their record cleared by God. There was a time when I wouldn't admit what a sinner I was. But my dishonesty made me miserable and filled my days with frustration. All day and all night my heart was heavy in me. My strength evaporated like water on a summer's day, until I finally admitted all my sins to you, and stopped trying to hide them. I said to myself, 'I will confess them to the Lord.' And you forgave me! All my guilt is gone. Now I say that each believer should confess his sins to God when he is aware of them, while there is time to be forgiven. Judgement will not touch him if he does' (Ps 31:1-6).

At the risk of stealing the last word from the psalmist, may I add the following as a sort of PS to this chapter? When you buy a machine of any kind, you will be well advised to follow the maker's instructions as you assemble it, wire it up, plug it in, or switch it on. To ignore those instructions could led to a blow-up or a break-down! I am convinced that part of the maker's instructions that comes with each human being is a strong plea for honesty and truth if full satisfaction is to be achieved.

Holiness

I decided to write about holiness immediately after writing about sin, repentance, and reconciliation, because I believe that the acid test of holiness is to have a deep and profound insight into my sinfulness; to be convinced beyond doubt that I need a power greater than myself. Holiness does not consist in working my way towards the Holy of Holies of the Lord, at the front of the temple – because that's where the Pharisee is. Holiness consists in looking at my life honestly, realising that I am more like the rest of men than I ever thought I was, and then making my way to join the publican in the lowest place at the back. He was the one who 'went away justified' (Lk 18:14). The closer I come to God the more obvious is the contrast; the brighter the light, the more evident the dust and the cobwebs. I could never understand how people like St Thérèse of Lisieux or Padre Pio could possibly be sincere when they referred to themselves aṣ 'great sinners' My inner response was to dismiss such comments as pietistic protestation from people whom I saw as never having committed a 'decent' sin in their lives! I'm beginning to see now, however, that their firm conviction about the reality of their claim was the foundation and the motivation of their holiness.

I'm sure you have often heard such expressions as 'that person is awfully scattered'; 'he is all over the place'; 'he badly needs to get himself together.' The opposite to that is togetherness, wholeness; a much nicer word for this is holiness. When you speak to a holy person you have that person's full attention, because she is together. The ability to give a total 'presence' to another is one of the proofs of holiness. (I'm speaking here of a very down-to-earth holiness, something we see in good people we meet – not a holiness that is so heavenly as to be no earthly good!)

One of the supporting pillars of love is listening. I cannot claim to love a person to whom I don't listen. A wholesome, holy person gives a total presence to the other, just as he does to God in prayer. By doing this he is confirming the other – you are important, I care about what you have to say, what you think, feel, etc. You feel very much at home with such a person because he is 'at home' in that body, he is in residence, he is 'all there'. Did you ever have the experience of speaking to someone for several minutes before you realised that his mind and attention are hundreds of miles away? I have a poster here on the wall before me as I write. It is a tombstone in a cemetery, and written on the tombstone are the words: 'Now you'll believe I was sick!' It would seem that someone had not been listening.

There is a very real and direct relationship between holiness and having a sense of sin, being really convinced that I am a sinner. If I really believed I was a sinner, I would become much more understanding and sympathetic towards others. Really believing that I certainly cannot afford to throw the first stone – that's a basis for holiness. Thanking God that I am like the rest of men, can do a great deal to curb my tendency to criticise or condemn others.

Holiness is what happens to me! God surrounds me with every single person, situation, and circumstance that will make me holy. I say, 'That one?' and God replies, 'Yes, she'll make you very patient.' 'That fellow?' 'Yes, he'll make you very forgiving.' There's not a person, a situation or a circumstance in my life that I can do without if I want to become holy. It is a great blessing, indeed, to look around me in life at everything that is part of it and then to stand up, amid all of it and say 'Yes', and bloom where I'm planted!

There once was a boy who decided he would

become a saint. He went down to the library and got out some books on saints, to see what kind of saint he would be. He read about Simon Stylites, who spent a lot of his time up on top of a huge column down in the town square. The boy thought that this was a good way to become a saint, because if you were going to go to all that trouble, then you may as well get as much publicity along the way as you can! There was no column around to climb up on, of course, so he decided to begin very simply. He got a chair in the kitchen, and he stood up on it. His sister came rushing in the back door, and nearly knocked him down. He moved the chair. His mother wanted to get to the sink, and he was in the way. He moved the chair. Someone wanted to get milk out of the fridge, and was unable to open the door because of the chair. After a while the boy, in disgust, just put the chair to one side and walked out the door with the remark, 'It's just impossible! It's just impossible to be a saint at home.' Sorry, son, it's not possible to become a saint anywhere else but where you are living! Bloom where you're planted.

I said earlier that holiness is what happens to me. It's not something I do. It's like my little niece who eventually got teeth and more hair, but she had to wait. There was nothing she could do but let it happen. There is a method, a clear and definite process to all of this. In other words, God knows what he is doing. I heard of a man who had a huge block of marble and he proceeded with hammer and chisel to sculpt an elephant. His friend came up to him and asked, 'How do you intend doing the job? I mean you're not a sculptor, and you really don't know anything about this kind of work, do you?' 'Well I don't actually, but I was thinking that I should just begin with hammer and chisel and chip off anything that doesn't look like an elephant.' There's a little more to it than that.

Henri Nouwen in his book *Clowning in Rome* relates an incident that is much closer to reality. A young lad was on his way to school. He was passing a sculptor's workshop and he looked in and saw a huge block of marble on which the sculptor was ready to begin work. The young lad had to keep going, and for months after that the front doors of the workshop were closed as he passed by, even though he could hear the sculptor at work inside. Then one day, as he was passing by, the front doors were open again; the boy looked in, and to his amazement, where the block of marble had been was a figure of a tiger. The young lad walked right up to the sculptor, tugged at his coat and asked, 'Excuse me, Sir, but how did you know there was a tiger in there?' When the Father looks at me he sees the image of his Son – but it take a great deal of chipping away and sandpaper treatment to produce the masterpiece.

For years I had the wrong idea about saints. To be a saint, I thought one had to be skinny! Some sort of undernourished ascetic-looking creature, who had neither a decent meal nor a good night's rest for years! And then to add to the image was the skeleton on the desk, in the picture, that gave a sort of ruthlessness to the very concept of holiness. I thought a saint was someone who went over to the person in the wheel-chair, said a prayer over him, and the invalid got up and walked. I had failed to realise that it is a sinner who does that sort of thing and if he exercises that kind of faith often enough he might become a saint some day. I thought I'd have to be a saint first.

In today's world, holiness is rarely equated with success. There is no easy road to holiness, no instant holiness. Becoming a saint is not just 'moving towards' but 'moving away from'. Becoming a saint is the long hard pull against the self-indulgent life, and towards that life of service. Holiness is open to sinners only. If you don't believe that then you have fooled yourself into believing that God created you to be an angel. In a sense we are possessed of dual-personalities – sinner and saint – one side leaning towards good, the other towards evil. Once a young lad who apparently felt these opposing forces within him, described himself as almost having a quadruple personality, when he admitted, 'Sometimes I'm bad, and sometimes I'm very bad. Sometimes I'm good and sometimes I'm very good.' And indeed, sometimes we are all of those things. But good or bad, very good or very bad, Jesus' invitation stands: 'Would you like to gain your life? Would you like to become a real success? Here's how...' And then he hands you the eight beatitudes – the secret of holiness.

In *The Power and the Glory*, Graham Greene tells of a priest who is condemned to death during an era of religious persecution in Mexico. The terrifying tensions of the priest's latter years had driven him to drink. 'It was the morning of his death. He crouched on the floor with the empty brandy flask in his hand, trying to remember an act of Contrition. "O God, I am sorry." He was confused – it was not the good death for which he had always prayed. He caught sight of his own shadow on the cell wall. What a fool he had been to think that he was strong enough to stay when others fled. "What an impossible fellow I am," he thought, "I have done nothing for anybody. I might just as well never have lived." Tears poured down his face; he was not at that moment afraid of damnation. He felt only an immense disappointment because he had to go to God emptyhanded, with nothing at all. It seemed to him at that moment that it would have been quite easy to have been a saint. It would have needed only a little self-restraint and a little courage. He felt like someone who had missed happiness by seconds at an appointed place. He knew now that at the end there was only one thing that counted – to be a saint.'

Whatever we may think of this man's chances of getting to heaven, we must agree with him on one point – the road to becoming a saint is a much easier one than the other road. I remember meeting a young man leaving a rehabilitation centre for alcoholics some years ago. He had come there only the day before, and he was walking out of there the very next morning. 'Do you know what they wanted me to do in there?' he confided in me in a shocked whisper. 'They wanted me to change my whole life-style!' The poor lad saw that as being far too difficult, and he was getting out of there as fast as he could. In fact, this man had chosen the more difficult road by far, and the road that had been suggested to him was much, much easier, and held hopes of so much more love, happiness, and life, than the one he chose to follow.

Faith

'What is faith?' It is the confident assurance that something we want is going to happen. It is the certainty that what we hope for is waiting for us, even though we cannot see it up ahead (Heb 11:1). Faith is acting now, and waiting for the proof later. If I got the proof first, there would be no need for faith. Atheists would have no problem in believing if they could be given the proof first. Faith now becomes vision later on. Faith is humility, knowing my place before God, having patience to wait for proof. 'You believe because you have seen,' Jesus told Thomas, 'Blessed are they who have not seen and yet believe' (Jn 20:29). Buying a new car, moving to a new job, going into hospital for an operation, walking to the altar to get married – these are all acts of faith, in so far as I act now and get the proof later.

Faith in Jesus is all of that and much more. Faith is a decision; it is a response to the offer of Jesus. Jesus didn't go around healing anyone. He went around with the power to heal, and the people themselves had to decide whether to respond to his offer or not. When they did so and were healed, they were told, 'your faith has made you well' (Lk 8:48). There were many many people in Galilee in Jesus' time who died of leprosy and other diseases, because they did not respond to his presence amongst them.

Faith is a response to love. If you really love someone you expect that person to trust you. Jesus came from the Father with a message of love – and the response he expected was one of faith. Such faith is in our feet, and not our heads! It enables us to step out and touch the hem of his garment. Such faith leads to action, simply because it is a response.

Paul says that we are saved by Jesus' blood and our faith (Rom 3:25). Trusting Jesus Christ to take away our sins is a necessary condition for getting to heaven, Paul says in that same chapter. Peter says that repenting and 'believing in the Lord Jesus' (Acts 2:38) is an essential ingredient for salvation. Jesus' promises are sure and certain. There is not one 'maybe' or one 'might' in the whole lot! Faith in Jesus Christ is trusting him totally to keep his promises. One of the loveliest tributes ever paid to Mary was that one of Elizabeth, 'All this happened to you because you believed that the promises of the Lord would be fulfilled' (Lk 1:45). You see, Mary was so humble, and had such a deep awareness of her own lowliness, that she saw herself with no choice but to believe. The apostles lacked a great deal in this area; that is why Jesus had to continually rebuke them as 'men of little faith' (Mt 6:30).

Faith is fundamental to the Christian life. It is basically a friendship between God and you, a felt relationship that grows like a grain of mustard seed if it is practised (Mt 17:20). I learned to walk by walking, to talk by talking – and to trust and believe by trusting and believing. Faith is a gift, of course, but, like any other gift, it must be nurtured and developed through use. A cartoon appeared in a recent magazine in which a mother and father are arguing over their son's budding musical career. 'All right,' the horrified father exclaims, 'so he'll grow up to be a tuba virtuoso. But can't he just take lessons? Does he have to practise?' Yes, indeed, he has to practise, and on the road to perfection it is true that practise makes perfect.

Faith means different things to different people. To some it is the content of their belief– like just another word to describe a denomination of religion, for example, the Catholic faith. What I am speaking of here is faith in Jesus Christ. This is so much more than just believing what he says. It is to believe in him, to trust him. In this sense faith is basically in the present – the vision and proof are in the future.

Faith in Jesus is believing that Jesus is alive, that he is living in me, and that he works in and through me. Because of this, then, faith is in my feet more than in my head; it enables me to step out and act on that. How I step out shows exactly just how real my faith is.

A man was climbing up the side of a mountain when he slipped and fell towards the jagged rocks below. He frantically grabbed a bush on the way down and, to his delight it, held him. He began to pray; 'O God, please, please help me.' A voice from above was heard to say, 'Do you believe I can help you?' 'Oh yes, Lord, I believe, I believe.' 'Do you believe I can save you from crashing onto those rocks below?' 'Oh, yes, Lord, I do, I do.' 'Do you really believe?' 'Oh, yes, Lord, I believe. I believe beyond a doubt.' 'OK, then – let go of that bush!' One version of that story ends with the man calling out, 'Is there anybody else up there?'

Faith is an attitude of total reliance on God's goodness. We can be right with God only by holding to the conviction that God is good. Our Irish grandmothers based their faith in God on a favourite saying of theirs; 'God is good – and he has a good mother.' Faith is a response to goodness, just like a child's response to loving and caring parents. There is a difference in attitude, not to mention output, between a son who does things for his father out of love and gratitude, and that of an employee who does things for pay, or out of fear that he may lose his job, or not get a promotion. What counts is motivation. If I accept God's goodness and love, then I will respond. The very approach of Jesus, his whole attitude towards us, and dealings with us, is calling for such a response. To hear his message, to receive his call is to respond with a deep faith and trust. 'Faith comes from hearing' (Rom 10:17). Not to believe is not to have really heard.

Faith is one of the gifts of the Holy Spirit; it is part of the power I get to do things. It is a free gift that is offered to me as being essential in doing the Lord's work. It differs somewhat from the *virtue* of faith, in so far as the *gift* of faith will be operational through me only when there is a specific need for it, when I am in a situation where this special charismatic gift is needed, for the sake of his Body. The virtue of faith, the response to the great love offered, must, however, precede the coming of the Holy Spirit. 'He sent his Holy Spirit, as his first gift to those who believe' we are told in Eucharistic Prayer IV. Faith is an essential foundation; without it nothing is helpful, nothing will take place. Not even going to Mass regularly, not even frequent prayer, not even being baptised. Faith is more important than any of these, and indeed, without it none of these has any value for us. It is the ground-work; it is the rock on which we build.

Three clergymen, a Jewish rabbi, a Protestant minister, and a Catholic priest were fishing together. They rowed to the middle of a small lake, dropped anchor, and cast their lines. Soon they ran out of bait. The rabbi volunteered to go for more. Calmly, he stepped off the boat, and walked across the water to shore. When he returned in the same manner, it was discovered that the trio's water cans were empty. The minister collected them, and, like the rabbi, walked across the water to shore and back. Later, when the men grew hungry, they realised they had forgotten their lunch basket. Whereupon the priest quickly rose, stepped off the boat, and immediately sank to the bottom of the lake! When he came to the surface, he heard the rabbi say to the minister, 'I suppose we should have told him where the stones are.' Faith is knowing that the stones are there before stepping out. Peter could have stayed in the boat and confessed Jesus to be the Son of God, but his faith was in his feet, so he stepped out. Unfortunately poor Peter's head took over, he took his eyes off Jesus, and he panicked. Had he kept his eyes on Jesus, and remembered his great love and care for him, he could have kept going. Faith is to be sure of that love – and to step out in confidence and trust.

Faith makes things possible, it doesn't make them easy. Faith must lead to action. In a general way I could say that God does nothing for me – I must do it, and he makes that possible. Did you ever hear of the man whose beard went on fire, and he prayed that it would start raining? Faith must never be an excuse for inactivity. 'Dear Brothers, what's the use of saying that you have faith, and are Christians, if you aren't proving it by helping others? Will that kind of faith save anyone? It isn't enough just to have faith. You must also do good and prove that you have it. Faith that doesn't show itself by good works is no faith at all; it is dead and useless' (Jas 2 14:17). If you really want to know what I believe in, then watch how I behave and act – that is my creed in action.

The Holy Spirit

The apostles answered Jesus' call to leave all things and follow him. They lived with him for three years, witnessed his power, and heard his teaching. They met him after the resurrection, when he repeated his promises, and he renewed their commission. And yet they remained locked in an upper room for fear of the people. Jesus had told them to 'remain in the city until the Holy Spirit comes' (Acts 1:4). It was only when the Holy Spirit came that the whole picture would fall into place, that they would be ready to really respond to his message. He told them in simple language to do nothing and to say nothing about his message until the Spirit came, because, until then, they wouldn't even know how to begin. He promised them 'You will be filled with power when the Holy Spirit comes to you, and you will be my witnesses in Jerusalem, in all of Judaea and Samaria, and to the ends of the earth' (Acts 1: 8). This is going to be his work, so he has promised to supply the power.

There are two parts to the whole story of salvation.

The first part is what Jesus did, and when he did that, he went away, and he hasn't come back yet. He sent the Holy Spirit to do the second part. This is essential to understand, if we are to accept our proper place in God's plan. The first part is what Jesus did. He then sent the Holy Spirit 'to complete his work on earth, and to bring us the fulness of grace', as we say in the prayer of the Mass. In simple language, my response to what Jesus did, is to allow the Holy Spirit take over, and complete the saving work of Jesus in me. Mary's glory consisted, not in anything she did, but in allowing the Holy Spirit do whatever he wanted in her, and with her.

Jesus considered the sending of his spirit to be the highest point of all that he had to do. It was the pinnacle of success for his mission. He even told his apostles that it was more important for them that the Spirit should come than that he should stay. 'But I tell you the truth; it is better for you that I go away, because if I do not go, the Holy Spirit will not come to you. But if I do go away I will send him to you' (Jn 16:2). He uses words of great promise when he refers to the Holy Spirit; he calls him the Comforter, the Helper, the Advocate. 'He will never leave you' (Jn 14:16). 'He will teach you all things, lead you into all truth, and make you remember all that I have told you'(Jn 14:26). He himself was often filled with the joy and ecstasy of the Spirit (Lk 10:21), and he then could offer his disciples: 'My joy will be in you', 'My peace I give you', – joy pressed down and flowing over.

Jesus had put his divinity aside, and it was only through the Spirit within him that he could speak and act with power. 'It is God's Spirit who gives me the power to drive out demons' (Mt 12:28). 'The Holy Spirit came upon him in bodily form like a dove' (Lk 3:22). 'Jesus returned from the Jordan, full of the Holy Spirit, and was led by the Spirit into the desert' (Lk 4:1). There is no doubting throughout the gospel where Jesus' power came from! Later on, he promised that those who believed in him would do even greater things, because he was going back to the Father, and would send the Holy Spirit (Jn 14: 12).

The Holy Spirit enables me to do things I could never do by myself. The eastern Church has usually been more aware of the Holy Spirit than have we in the west. In *Dialogues with Patriarch Athenagoros* we read this splendid summary of the importance of the Holy Spirit:

> Without the Holy Spirit, God is far away, Christ stays in the past, the gospel is a dead letter, the Church is simply an organisation, authority a matter of domination, mission a matter of propaganda, the liturgy no more than an invocation, Christian living a slave morality. But in the Holy

Spirit the cosmos is resurrected, and groans with the birthpangs of the kingdom, the risen Christ is there, the gospel is the power of life, the Church shows forth the life of the Trinity, authority is a liberating service, mission is a Pentecost, the liturgy is both memorial and anticipation, human action is deified. In simple language, the Holy Spirit makes all the difference in the world. . .

Jesus rose from the dead on Easter Sunday. It was the day of his triumph, the 'day that the Lord has made, let us rejoice and be glad in it.' Once a kid said to me, 'So Jesus rose from the dead – good for him! But what good is that for me; I can't get out of bed in the morning!' Yes, indeed, if it is just something that happened to Jesus, then it could simply be a fact of history. However, it is so much more than that. Whatever happened to Jesus on Easter Sunday is made available to all of us – and that is called Pentecost, the coming of the Holy Spirit. That coming is like the breath that is spoken of in Ezekiel, which gave life to the dry bones, and created a living army of people (Ezek 37:14). Earlier in Ezekiel we read God's promises, 'And I will give you a new heart, I will give you new and right desires, and put a new spirit within you. I will take out your stony hearts of sin and give you new hearts of love. And I will put my Spirit within you, so that you will obey my laws and do whatever I command' (Ezek 36:26-32). When we speak of the

Holy Spirit coming, we speak of entering into a whole new way of life.

At the time of creation the Spirit of God hovered over the waters, bringing order out of chaos. God's creation is continuous, as the Spirit continues to create order out of chaos. Cardinal Suenens says, 'I believe that God is new every morning; I believe that God is creating the world today, at this very moment. He did not just create it in the long ago, and then forget about it.' 'Send forth your Spirit and we shall be created, and you shall renew the face of the earth,' is the prayer of the Church. Where the Holy Spirit is, there is always new life, revelation, and resurrection hopes. The Holy Spirit is diametrically opposed to the spirits of despair, of inactivity, or of lethargy.

There is a story of a man who felt such despair about life that he climbed up on a bridge to commit suicide. A policeman came along to get him down. As the policeman inched his way towards him, he succeeded in striking a bargain with him. 'I'll give you ten minutes to tell me what's wrong with the world, and why you want to end it all. Then you give me ten minutes to tell you what's right with the world, why you should go on living.' The man began to tell what he thought of the world, and was in full flight when the policeman had to stop him, because he was gone well over his ten minutes. Then it was the policeman's turn. He began to tell what was right with the world; he was humming and hawing, and soon ran out of things to say. He thought to himself for a moment, looked again at the other man, reached out and took him by the hand – and they both jumped off together! The Spirit of God, who teaches us all things and brings us into all truth, as Jesus promised, gives me all the reasons for living, and for living to the full.

After Pentecost, Peter might well have asked Jesus, 'Why didn't you give me this Holy Spirit long ago, and not have me making a fool of myself, cutting off that man's ear, half-drowning myself, or letting you down at the question of a servant girl?' And Jesus would have smiled and said, 'You weren't ready at all, Peter. You were too full of yourself. You didn't believe for one moment that you needed the Holy Spirit. You are one of those people who has to learn everything the hard way.' It was only when the apostles came to a deep realisation that they really did need the power, that they were ready to go into the upper room and wait for it. I myself find that it is much easier to speak to broken people, to recovering alcoholics, to social failures, about the power of the Holy Spirit, than to those who have not really experienced their own brokenness and weakness.

We are like reluctant chicks fearfully peeping out

from the place of our incubation. The Spirit comes to shatter the shells, and to invite us out into the great world where Christ is making all things new. The venture to which he invites us is the venture for which he empowers us. There is great symbolism in the idea of the apostles pouring out of that upper room – free men, men with a message, men with a mission. Jesus has come again – in great power this time, and not as a helpless babe.

When Jesus went away, he sent his Holy Spirit, and he asked our co-operation by providing the Body. There was no body anymore, and so it was essential that we love one another, and that we be one, so that the world might believe, that the message might be credible (Jn 17:21). A Spirit needs a body to do and to say and to go. The Spirit supplies the power, the words, the inspiration. I could have a spirit of generosity, but that spirit needs my hands to put that generosity into action! Central to our vocation as Christians is to provide the Body, in family, prayer group, parish etc.

When Paul met a small group of people in Ephesus who had accepted the Christian message, his first question to them was, 'Did you receive the Holy Spirit when you became believers ?' They replied, 'No, we were never even told there was such a thing as a Holy Spirit' (Acts 19:2-3). I can almost imagine Paul smiling, because if you received the

Holy Spirit you would know it, and so would everyone else! These people had repented and were converted, but they had not expressed faith in the full Christian message. It is the Holy Spirit who is the fullness and perfection of the message of Jesus. It was to gain this fullness that Jesus came, and as John the Baptist told his followers, 'The man on whom you see the Spirit come down and rest, is the one who is going to baptise with the Holy Spirit' (Jn 1:34). This phrase sums up the whole purpose of Jesus' coming, namely that every one of us would be born again in the Spirit, and receive the life-giving power of God in our mortal bodies. It is this that makes Christianity different from every other religious system – the presence of the power of God through his Holy Spirit.

Living: Walking in the Spirit

'Learn to walk and to live in the Spirit,' says Paul (Gal 5-25). When I ask God for something he will want to know: 'Why do you want this? For yourself or for others? If for others and their good, if for the good of Christ's Body, the Church, then certainly. You want peace? Why? So that you will feel good and be able to sit back, relax, and have a nice time? If that's why you want peace, then you won't get it. You want peace so that you can share it with others? Oh, surely, plenty of it.'

I believe that when I am ready to walk and live in the Holy Spirit I am ready to receive the Holy Spirit. I cannot ask for the Holy Spirit first, and then decide what to do with him! The Holy Spirit is not given to an individual, he is given to the Church, and, therefore, those people who have accepted an active responsible role within the Body of the Church are the ones who are open to the Spirit.

I was baptised and confirmed, therefore I have the Holy Spirit. But the Holy Spirit may not have me! I don't know much about gardening, but if I saw a tree with apples on it I could safely presume it to be an apple tree. When I look at your life and see the fruits of the Spirit – love, joy, peace, etc. – I know you have the Holy Spirit; if the evidence is not there, I could very well ask you whatever happened the Holy Spirit you received? Of course I was baptised and confirmed, but sooner or later I must take responsibility for that, I must say my own 'yes.' This is what is often called 'Baptism in the Spirit'. It is not a sacrament, and may be received as often as I wish. It is a coming into an experience of something I had all the time. It is a personal investment in my own spiritual life, a coming-of-age, a time of mature decision. I must be baptised in the Spirit, I must have my pentecost – when the lights come on, the coin drops, and my best suspicions of Jesus are confirmed. This moment, this experience, this personal acceptance of Jesus in the totality of himself and his message – this is something that is necessary for all Christians. In fact, I myself believe that only at this point does my Christianity really begin. St Teresa of Avila says that her conversion to Christianity took place at the age of thirty-eight, after twenty years spent in a convent!

What does it mean to walk and live in the Spirit? It means entering a whole new way of life, a life where the conditions have changed since the days when I walked and lived in the flesh. Let me put it this way. Suppose your boss was mean, unjust, rude, and tyrannical. He never missed an opportunity to humiliate and torment you. You were continually under supervision and suspicion, and you never got a break. One day another man comes into the place where you work. He feels sorry for you, and believes you deserve something better. He offers you an opportunity to get away from your present position of slavery, and go and work for him. He gives you a post of responsibility, a position that has dignity, and in which you are free to be a positive and helping agent in the lives of many others. Things are going along grand, until one day your former boss walks in and proceeds to berate and humiliate you as of old. Would you accept this from him now? Would you not rather tell him very definitely that you owe him nothing, that he has no longer any rights over you, that you are now free? Order him out, and send him packing to where he came from. You are now living and walking in the power of the Spirit, and Satan no longer has any claim on you. He will, of course, continue to try to bully you, to dominate you, to control you. Walking and living in the Spirit means being free – and staying free. It means making use of your new-found power and authority which Jesus, living in you, makes available and possible.

Walking and living in the Spirit means walking and living in the power of the Spirit. It is Jesus's work we are engaged in – 'to complete his work on earth' – therefore it can only be done by his power. Jesus wants us to use power tools, which are the gifts of the Spirit. I can use an electric saw, which is plugged in, and the saw is working by a power which is not mine. That's the kind of power Jesus wants us to avail of. 'All power in heaven and on earth is given to me' (Mt 28 :1819).

A very holy man, who had served for many years in a big city parish, decided to shift gear in middle age by settling down as a parish priest among a small rural congregation. This happened many years ago, but this is the way he still tells the story of his first big country meal in a parishioner's home. 'The eating was so good it was almost sinful: roast beef, baked ham, and fried chicken, mashed potatoes, vegetable casseroles, fresh baked bread rolls, etc. All through the meal something was bothering me. I just couldn't enjoy it. All during the dinner I heard the obvious sound of running water, and it really bugged me. Back in the city that sound was bad news, someone had left a tap running, and the sink or the bath was about to overflow; or there was a leak in the plumbing; the ceiling was about to cave in. For two hours I heard little else but the sound of running water.

However, since it was my first visit to this parishioner's home, I was reluctant to say anything. Finally, I could hold out no longer so I asked about it. With a smile my host explained the situation to me. It seems that forty years before, when the people had built the farm-house, they discovered a spring of water right in the centre of their property. So they built a fountain and reservoir around it, and designed the house around the fountain. For forty years the people who lived in the house had been refreshed and nourished by the spring of water that was welling up right at the centre of their home. I thought to myself, "That is what Jesus is constantly trying to tell us: that it is possible for us to build the rooms of our lives around the life-giving water spring of his Spirit."' 'If you only knew what a wonderful gift God had for you, and who I am, you would ask me for living water … the water I give becomes a perpetual spring within them, watering them for ever with eternal life' (Jn 4:10-14).

Baptism in the Holy Spirit is simply coming into an experience of something I had all the time. It is something I have to experience, and understand later. If I insist on trying to understand it first, I'm in trouble. I remember an old sister some years ago who helped me understand this in a very tangible way. She was ninety-three years of age and in full possession of all her faculties. I had just given a talk to the community, and was having a cup of coffee, when she walked right into the parlour where I was. I had been speaking about the baptism in the Spirit, and her question was direct and simple: 'Father whatever it is you're talking about, I want it, I want it all, and I want it now!' No further questions, no further comment. I brought her down the corridor to a small prayer room where the blessed sacrament was exposed, and I got her to say those same words to Jesus 'Lord, whatever it is you're talking about I want it, I want it all, and I want it now.' After over seventy years, and years of retreats, of courses in religious studies, of living in a religious community, she had at last got down from her sycamore tree and prepared to meet Jesus on his terms. It was a very real conversion for someone who already had walked with the Lord. I prayed with her, the Lord touched her deep in the core of her being, and she began to cry like a child. The following day at the closing Mass of the retreat, as the sisters were sharing prayers after Communion, her prayer was really moving, as she prayed, 'Now thou dost dismiss they servant in peace, O Lord, because my eyes have seen your salvation.' She died a week later. It took her ninety-three years to arrive at this stage, but it was worth every day of it.

I said earlier that the whole gospel is summed up in one basic truth: God loves me. I receive the fullness of the Spirit when I am so convinced of that love that I say my unconditional 'Yes' to God – the 'Fiat' of Mary, 'Be it done unto me according to thy word.' Only then will 'the Holy Spirit come upon me, and the power of the Most High overshadow me.' John writes in his first letter: 'We need have no fear of someone who loves us perfectly: his perfect love for us eliminates all dread of what he might do to us. If we are afraid, it is for fear of what he might do to us, and shows that we are not fully convinced that he really loves us' (1 Jn 4:18). No wonder we say that a saint is not the person who loves God, but the person who is fully convinced that God loves him.

To live and walk in the Spirit is to be a person of power. 'Dear young friends, you belong to God, and have already won your fight with those who are against Christ, because there is someone in your hearts who is stronger than any evil teacher in this wicked world' (1 Jn 4:4). When I live and walk in the Spirit I can expect that the gifts of the Spirit will be available when needed. As I counsel someone, I expect to have discernment, wisdom, and knowledge, because this is God's work, and he guarantees to supply the power. As the person leaves my room, I may not know what day it is!

The gifts are not personal possessions, and are available only while needed for the sake of building up the Body. In the actual living out of my Christian life I can expect all of the gifts to be active in my life at some time or another, and most of the time I don't even know it! It is not necessary that I know, because these are not personal gifts, their presence is no indication of personal merit or holiness. It is the fruits of the Spirit that have to do with personal holiness.

Baptism in the Spirit, which brings the availability of the gifts of the Spirit, is like the vertical bar on a cross. It is something between God and me. Baptism of fire, which produces the fruits of the Spirit, is like the horizontal bar, when I begin to reach out to others as the Lord has reached down to me, when I begin to love others as Jesus has loved me. This baptism of fire will burn away layers and layers of selfishness. Baptism in the Spirit with the gifts is like the tree in the gospel, with beautiful foliage, but no fruit! Because it continued to produce only leaves and no fruit, Jesus cursed it, and it withered.

The Cross/Suffering

I wrote in an earlier chapter that there are two parts to the history of salvation – the part Jesus did, and the part the Holy Spirit does, which, of course, is to complete the work of Jesus. To speak about the cross we must speak about what Jesus did. Jesus came down on this earth, and he opened up a path, a way, that leads us safely through the jungle of life. If we follow that path, that way, it will lead us home to the Father.

We call this the way, Jesus called himself the way, and members of the early Christian Church were known as followers of the way. This is a very clear, well-defined, and definite way, and the cross is the authentic mark and characteristic of this. Jesus says quite simply that if we want to be his disciples, then we must take up our cross every day and follow him. No room for doubt in these words!

Let me clarify what is meant by the cross in Christian language, so as to ensure there is no doubt or ambiguity whatever in our understanding. We sometimes refer to a handicapped child, a

crippling stroke, or some natural disaster as being a
'great cross' for those concerned. Without wishing
to appear callous or unfeeling, but with a sincere
desire for clarity and understanding of something
of great importance, I do not accept that these are
crosses. Not of themselves, that is. The cross is the
preserve of the Christian, and all of these things
can and do happen to pagans and atheists as well.
These can, of course, be sources of blessing, but not
necessarily. They could bring great holiness to one
person, and deep bitterness and resentment to
another. The cross, on the other hand, is always a
blessing, is always redemptive.

What, then, is the cross, in the Christian understanding of the word ? When I decide to walk the
Christian way, to follow the footsteps of Jesus,
everything, but everything I do after that is a cross.
I have to forgive, to share, to listen, to pray. I have
no choice anymore. I must take up my cross every
day, and stop looking for easy options, for an easy
way out. The Christian way is not an easy way.
There is no easy way, and yet his way is the only
way in which I will find happiness. Yes, indeed, his
burden is sweet and light and we do find rest for
our souls.

To love Jesus is to obey him (Jn 14:15). Fear of the
cross, of what it may cost me, may well limit my
obedience. Jesus obeyed the Father totally, and his

very meat was 'to do the will of him who sent me' (Jn 4:34). Jesus would then turn to us and say, 'As the Father sent me, so I am sending you'. Your love for me will be shown through your obedience. There is a cost in Pentecost, there is no easy way. Real Christian living is to embrace the cross, to come to love the cross, never to run away when the price seems too high. The road to heaven is heaven, even though, to someone of a worldly mind-set, it may look more like hell! On the other hand, the foolish may believe that the road to hell is heaven! Oh no, indeed, to be allowed walk with Jesus and share his cross for the salvation of the world, is a joy and a privilege that only the Spirit of God could reveal.

The cross is the sign of our salvation. In its vertical and horizontal bars it combines the human and the divine, the God and man in Jesus, our saviour. It is more than just an ornament, a symbol, a Christian coat of arms. It is a banner of victory over sin, sickness, and death. When the cross is not understood properly it is thought of as a burden, a dark cloud, something to be feared, rather than a banner of victory. It is the key that unlocks the tomb, that opens the door to the kingdom. 'To the Jews it is a stumbling-block, to the Gentiles it is foolishness, but for those whom God has called, both Jews and Gentiles, it is the power and the wisdom of God'

(Cor 1:23-24). The power and the wisdom of God. No wonder it is something to be avoided at all costs by the world!

There can be a big difference between sickness and suffering. Suffering is redemptive, cleansing, purifying. Suffering is always accompanied by the grace to carry that cross. When I visit someone in hospital who is suffering, I will be welcomed, asked how I am, how my work is going, and so on; and it may be some time before it dawns on me that all of this is from a person in a hospital bed. Redemptive suffering takes out the very best in the person who is called on to bear it. It is truly charismatic, because we are the ones who really benefit from it. In the body, if one member does not function then another member must take over; if I cannot see, then my hands, as they grope along, and my ears as they sense every sound and movement, must do my seeing for me. In a hedonistic and pleasure-seeking society, where there is a tablet or a bottle for every human pain, ache, problem, or inconvenience, then someone must carry the cross. I believe that our psychiatric hospitals are full of people who are carrying the cross for the rest of us. Throughout salvation there have always been holy innocents whose blood was redemptive for others.

Sickness, on the other hand, can be quite different from suffering. I visit someone in hospital who is sick and am given a detailed list of pains, aches, worries, anxieties and complexities; and I myself would be mistaken if I expected any enquiry or interest about myself, or my health. It is difficult to see how this is from God. 'By their fruits you shall know them,' says Jesus, and it is sometimes impossible to see any good fruit resulting from a lot of sickness. I believe this is faith or non-faith all over again; I respond to a loving God, or I get wrapped up in myself. The actual physical complaint can be exactly similar, but in one case it is a sickness, and in another it is redemptive suffering.

There were once two young boys. One was a pessimist, the other was an optimist. The pessimist was put into a room filled with toys, the optimist was put into a room filled with manure from the farmyard, and the doors were closed on them. An hour later they were checked on. The pessimist was sitting on the floor in the midst of all the toys, and he was crying. His reason? There was no drum! The optimist, on the other hand didn't hear the door being opened, as he was so busy. He had a small shovel, and he was busy shovelling the manure to the other corner of the room, while his eyes popped with excitement and expectation. His reason? With all that manure, he was convinced there just had to be a pony there somewhere!

There is no short-cut or bypass from Holy

Thursday to Easter Sunday. The cross is part of the Christian way of life. 'Anyone who wants to follow me must take up his cross every day,' says Jesus (Lk 9:23). The daily cross is not always a heavy one; as often as not it is merely the very pain of being human, the splinters of trying to love others as I ought. It involves dying, which is the greatest way to love another (Jn 15:13) – dying to my selfishness, my possessions, my pride, as I give new life to others. The Christian is asked to do his dying during his life-time. Death is like a pile of sand at the end of my life that I am asked to take and sprinkle throughout my daily living, so that when I come to the end there will be nothing there. If, on the other hand, I wait until the end of my life to die, it will be too late. My dying should be done by then. I have to die anyhow, but I have a choice. Like Jesus I can say, 'No one takes my life from me; I lay it down willingly' (Jn 10:15). As I walk through life towards the resurrection, cross in hand, I am getting on with the job of dying. Because I want to sit in Jesus' kingdom, I am willing to drink the cup which he drinks (Mt 20:22), to share in his suffering, to make up what is lacking in the sufferings of Christ.

We are always in a process of change. We have all seen cocoons hanging from trees and bushes in the Spring. The cocoon is protection for a working creature in the process of maturing into a butterfly.

The beauty and grace of the butterfly is wondrous to behold, but full maturity does not come without a struggle. Biologists have discovered that the struggle to break through the cocoon of old life into new life is absolutely necessary for the butterfly's survival. Without the struggle, the tiny wing muscles would not develop the strength required to fly free. Without the struggle, the butterfly would die in the cocoon. Cardinal Suenens says, 'Happy are those who dream dreams and are prepared to pay the price to make their dreams come true.' Another Cardinal, Newman, said that to live is to change and to become perfect is to have changed often.

Every one of us is just a heartbeat away from death. This becomes a threat to us, and a threat to the God who created us for life. It is there on the cross. It was a real death. It wasn't an imitation death or charade. One of the reasons the gospel writers want us to understand this is that by facing death, by confronting it honestly and realistically, we will be prepared for life. 'Death comes for us all my Lord,' says Thomas More in *A Man for all Seasons*. 'Death comes for us all. Even for kings he comes. Nor will he bow down nor pay them any reverence, but grab them by the breast and shake them 'till they're dead. Death comes for us all, my Lord.' Jesus wasn't brought back to life; Lazarus was – he still had to die; death was still a reality for him.

Jesus passed through death into a life in which death is non-existent, and he invites us to join him there today. As the Hebrews marked the doorposts of their houses so that the angel of death and destruction passed by, and left them unharmed, so I am marked with the life-giving sign of the cross, the victory sign of the Christian, and death has lost its sting. 'O death where is your victory? Where then is your sting?' (1 Cor 15:55).

For us the way of the cross is the path we must travel towards the Jerusalem that is more than a reality of politics or geography, towards the Jerusalem that is the symbol of the kingdom of God. We press on in the confident hope that, at the end, lies the New Jerusalem, the land of our fulfilment. Like Simon of Cyrene, we too will be offered the rare and beautiful privilege of putting our shoulders to the cross along the way. Praise God for the sharing!

Mary

No matter what I read or hear about Mary, the Mother of Jesus, the one thought that means most to me is: Whatever it is I am trying to do in response to God's call, Mary did it perfectly. Her openness to the Holy Spirit was the natural result of a very deep humility. When you really know that, by yourself, you just cannot do a particular thing, then you are much more open to receiving help from a greater power. When Mary's question, 'How can this be done?' was answered with an assurance that it would be done through the power of the Holy Spirit, then, of course, she banished all fear, all further questionings, and bowed her head in quiet acceptance. Mary's glory consists, not in anything she herself actually did, but in the fact that she allowed God do anything he wanted to do.

Mary is not the centre of Christianity, as some might be accused of making her out to be, but she certainly leads directly to the centre, and is always found at the centre. She points to Jesus and says, 'Whatever he says, you do' (Jn 2:5). Mary is found with the friends of Jesus, out at the edge of the crowd, and Jesus is in the centre (Mt 18:46). She has a very special mission in bringing people to Jesus, and Jesus to people; in building a deep and lasting relationship between her first child, and the rest of her children.

Mary was a woman of deep faith. Each one of us would be permanently transformed for the good if we only believed the good news that we hear. Mary heard, and she believed. 'All of this happened to you because you believed that God would do what he said,' was Elizabeth's greeting to her (Lk 1:45), and when it had passed from the head down into the heart, she accepted it totally. The word could then become flesh.

Yes, indeed, whatever it is we are called to do and to be, Mary is a perfect and clear model. She was totally emptied of pride and self-seeking, and God could therefore fill her with his Spirit. Her co-operation with that Spirit made it possible for Jesus to come on this earth. She became the first Christian as she brought Jesus to Elizabeth, Simeon, Anna, and Cana in Galilee. I often think of her visit to Elizabeth as a very simple, clear and beautiful example of Christianity in practice. She brought Jesus into that situation, and the whole stress was on the greatness and goodness of the Lord, and what great things he was doing. I might note, in passing, that, in a world of abortion on demand, it is so beautiful to think of the unborn John the Baptist leaping for joy in the presence of Jesus. God forgive us all if we deny the basic right to life to the unborn.

Jesus said, 'I will not leave you orphans' (Jn 14:18). Jesus never makes a statement which is totally unsupported and unconnected. When he said he wouldn't leave us orphans he was speaking against the background of his other statements, 'When you pray say, "Our Father" (Mt 6:9), and "Son, behold your Mother" (Jn 19:27) and "You must become like little children" (Mk 10:15). In other words, we are invited into the family of God – nothing less than full membership is offered. When I was born I became a part of my natural family. I had no choice, and we were stuck with each other. To become a member of God's family, however, I have to make a choice. When I do make this choice I am then born again, as Jesus explained to Nicodemus (Jn 3:3). Essential to being part of the family, of course, is my full acceptance of a God whom I can call *Abba* or daddy, and of a mother who takes me just as seriously as she did her first-born. The night before Jesus died, he gave himself in eucharist; a few minutes before he died he gave me his mother. John acknowledged and accepted the gift, and from that moment the disciple took her to his own (Jn 19:27). What a great pity if, two thousand years later, I was still a spiritual orphan, or a member of a spiritual one-parent family, with no mother!

After Jesus had entrusted us, represented by John, to the care of his mother at the foot of the cross, the evangelist then writes 'And then, all things having been accomplished' (Jn 19:28). In a beautiful, sensitive way he had thought of everything. It was now only a matter of waiting for the Spirit to come, and his work would be complete. He still had need for his mother; there was still work for her to do. Because of her own unique openness to the Spirit, she was the ideal person to conduct a special novena for Pentecost. She had something that rough pragmatists like Peter, or moody doubters like Thomas, needed very much. It may well have been difficult for Peter and Thomas. After a few days when nothing was happening in that upper room, poor Peter probably wanted to go home. He always had to be doing something, like jumping out of a boat and half drowning himself, or cutting off someone's ear and then running away! In the meantime, Thomas may well have been demanding proof that something was going to happen, or he would be off too! And then again poor Peter was somewhat a chauvinist and may have found it difficult to be told what to do by a woman! Someone once asked me if there might have been any connection between Peter's denial of Jesus, and Jesus' earlier healing of Peter's mother-in-law! Anyhow, Mary's quiet waiting prayer, her unassuming, but unshakeable, belief in God's promises, spoke louder to them than any words. Because of Mary they waited, prepared for, and received their Pentecost. In a way, Mary had given birth to Jesus once again. On this occasion, her co-operation with the Spirit resulted in the birth of the Church, the Body of Christ. She is the mother of the Church, and as a member of the Church I am naturally part of her family.

Sometimes Roman Catholics' emphasis on the role of Mary would seem to make her almost a co-redeemer with Jesus. In fact, it might also be implied that Mary could succeed in obtaining favours for you that even God himself would refuse! All of this would be a sad distortion of the truth, and it doesn't make for a proper understanding and appreciation of Mary at all. If this is what comes across, then I can truly sympathise with my fellow Christians in other Churches who are turned off Mary because of the wrong emphasis they seem to witness in some Roman Catholic circles. I have said twice already in this chapter that Mary did perfectly whatever it is I am called to do in response to God's call. There is little to add to that central truth, but I must come to an appreciation of how she can help me in my response, and why she would want to help me.

My natural mother was a central instrument in giving me life, and a powerful influence and help in my living out that life. She could not, however, live my life for me, and I'm sure she wouldn't want to. While a natural parent, in a way, must work towards redundancy, and is really successful only when her children don't need her anymore, Mary is, of course, never redundant in the spiritual life. We continue to ask her, and depend on her, to be with us, and to pray for us now and at the hour of our death.

Mary was the first altar of sacrifice in the new covenant. She truly could say of Jesus, 'This is my Body!' She shared Eucharist with Elizabeth, with Simeon and with Anna. She walked to Calvary and stood at the foot of the cross to get clear, graphic, and definite evidence of the horror of sin, the extent of divine forgiveness, and the depth of divine love. Mary holds Jesus out to me. Sometimes he's a helpless infant, and I recoil at the knowledge of my own weaknesses and limitations. Sometimes he's dead on the cross, and I shudder at the thought of the dying that is inherent in Christian living. Sometimes she holds out the Christ of pentecost, the Church – often really frustrating and uninspiring in its ordinariness. But there is no other Jesus, and she knows it. 'When people say, Look, here is Christ! or He is there! do not believe them' (Mt 24:23). If you keep a place for Mary in your life, you will never have any trouble recognising the authentic Christ. During Vatican II Karl Rahner SJ was asked what had happened to devotion to Mary in the Catholic Church. His answer was direct and simple: 'Unfortunately, many Catholics have allowed Christianity to become a set of abstractions or ideas, and abstractions don't need a mother.' Yes, indeed, as long as we remember that Christianity is about a person, Jesus Christ, then there will always be a place and a need for his mother.

One of the most important roles of Mary is to stand guard over her children and protect them from Satan. Even Jesus was tempted, but Mary was completely free even of an approach from Satan. She would crush his head and he would lie in wait for her heel (Gen 3:15). This role of Mary is so obviously important in today's world that I will hold it over and develop it at greater length in the next chapter.

Satan

Let me begin this chapter by summarising chapter twelve of the Book of Revelation (the last book in the bible). The great red dragon (Satan) was waiting for the woman (Mary) to give birth, so that he could devour the child (Jesus). God saved the child, and brought the woman to a place of safety. This led to a war in heaven, and Satan and all his armies were cast down to earth. Satan continued to persecute and torment the woman, and when this proved useless, he set out to attack the rest of her children – all who were keeping God's commandments and confessing that they belonged to Jesus (Rev 12:17). Four times in this passage there is reference to Satan being cast down to this earth. Later on, when Jesus came, he would refer to Satan as the prince of this world (Jn 16:11). It was to do battle with Satan that Jesus came. It was essential then, that Mary, the channel of his coming, should be totally free from any influence or contact with Satan.

Satan was, of course, defeated by Jesus. As Mary's

greatest richness was her total humility, so Satan's greatest driving force is his pride. He would never accept defeat, especially the humiliation of knowing that a mere human (Mary) was part of the power that defeated him. He could never forgive God for such an indignity. And so he fights on. Towards the end of time, Satan will be given a free hand once again for a brief time (2 Thess 2), but even then his powers will be greatly curtailed. He will completely fool those who are on their way to hell, because they have already said 'no' to the truth; they have refused to believe it and love it, and let it save them, so God will allow them to believe lies with all their hearts, and all of them will be justly judged for believing falsehood, refusing the truth, and enjoying their evil ways (2 Thess 2:10-12). In other words he has no influence over those who belong to Jesus.

This protection from Satan is very much part of Jesus' intention for us. I remember some years ago, we were familiar with ads for sausages which claimed that they were double-wrapped for double protection. In a way that describes us as well. Jesus says, 'I have given you full authority over all the power of the evil one. Nothing shall harm you' (Lk 10:19). To ensure the double protection, he then entrusts us to the care of his mother.

Satan was cast down to this earth, which then

became his kingdom. When Jesus came on earth, he came to take on Satan, and to defeat him. Satan has come in pride and disobedience, so Jesus came in humility and obedience. As soon as Jesus was filled with the Holy Spirit at the Jordan, he was led by the Spirit into the desert where he was tempted by the devil (Lk 4:1-2). It was by the power of God's Spirit that Jesus drove out demons (Mt 12:28), and he never missed an opportunity to do so. Later on, he would assure us that, when the Holy Spirit came on us, we too would have that power, and even greater (Jn 14:12). My authority over Satan, of course, depends on the authority I allow Jesus have over me.

The only advantage Satan has is in numbers. On his side are all those who are deliberately committed to evil, plus all those who have not made any decision, one way or another. There are three groups of people in this world: a small group who cause things to happen, a larger group who watch things happening, and a much larger group who never have a clue what's happening. With Jesus, you are either for him or against him. There's no in-between. Once a man was going to a Hallow-e'en party dressed in the costume of a devil. On his way, the heavens opened, and the rain was such that he dashed into a church for shelter. There was quite a crowd at a prayer meeting in the church, and his entrance created total panic, and sent people dashing for the exits. One old lady caught her coat-tail on the corner of a pew, and, as the man approached her, she pleaded, 'Satan, please, Satan – I've been coming to this church every day for the past sixty years – I admit that– but I just want you to know that during all of that time I was really on your side.'

Jesus prayed that we might be one (Jn 17:11), he asked the Father to keep us safe from Satan's power (Jn 17:15), and he promised that those who follow him would not walk in darkness, but would have the light of life (Jn 12:46). The hallmark of Satan is darkness and confusion. Life is a journey toward the vision of God. I have God, but I don't yet have the vision. The nearest I can come to seeing God in this life is whenever I come across a group of people who are united, and who love one another. Those people who contribute to confusion, division, and conflict, are doing the work of Satan. Goodness will always be opposed by evil, and evil is most insidious when it is disguised as good. Satan can change himself into an angel of light, so it is no wonder his servants can do it too, and seem like godly masters (2 Cor 11:14-15). No wonder Jesus warns us to be on our guard, and to watch and pray, lest we enter into temptation (Lk 22: 40).

I must always use the authority that Jesus gives me. I heard of a woman whose day began going wrong from the first waking moments. Whatever himself said he shouldn't have said it! The husband was expert at detecting the mood, so he slipped off to work quietly and quickly. Not so the children. Junior was still doing his homework in the middle of the breakfast cereal, another couldn't find socks, while another had gone back to sleep again! The tension was mounting. They were unceremoniously thrown out the door to school, to snap at their friends in turn, and to annoy the teachers by their lack of attention, all due to a carry-over of the upset of that morning. Meanwhile at 11.00 am our poor mother is still in the dressing-gown, pouring her tenth cup of tea, and lighting her tenth cigarette! It was just one of those mornings! Suddenly she realised, with horror, what had happened. Nothing that happened in her house that morning could possibly have come from God. This shocked her. She prayed, claimed the authority of the name of Jesus, and the power of his precious blood over everything and anything in the house that was not from him. The cloud lifted, she regained her calm, and then phoned her husband and reassured him it was safe to come home! If she had forgotten that she had that authority she may well have ended up on librium, valium, or alcohol by that evening.

Satan is the father of lies, he is the master of deceit. He is not capable of telling the truth. That is why Jesus lays such store on truth. He himself is the truth (Jn 14:6) and he assures us that, if we follow the truth, it will set us free (Jn 8:32). Satan loves the darkness, and he will try anything to prevent us living in the light. Bringing areas of darkness in my life to the healing and forgiveness of Jesus' love and light is to totally frustrate Satan's plans for us.

Another effective weapon of Satan is to convince us to put off to some other time something that we should do now. Perhaps a story might best illustrate this. Satan rounded up all his evil spirits from all over the world, and began a major conference to plan some new approaches against the Spirit of renewal that is so effective today among God's people. He ranted and raged against their fall-off in success, and demanded a think-in to come up with some urgent and effective plans for today's world. They put on their thinking caps. Eventually one devil stood up and said he had a plan. He was brought to the front to put his plan to the assembly: Why don't we go back up there and tell them that there's no such place as hell at all. Then they would really get reckless and irresponsible, and we would be back in business. This was greeted with loud applause from all except Satan himself, who shook his head, and said: That shows you don't know human beings at all, if you think they would buy that line of talk. Why, even their dogs look guilty when they do something wrong! This conscience thing is too much part of their make-up; they know when they've done wrong, and they are capable of sensing the reality of hell through their guilt, even during their life-times. No, I'm afraid you'll have to come up with a better plan than that one. Another long pause. Another devil steps forward to put his plan to the assembled gathering: Why don't we go up and tell them that there is a hell, but there's no heaven! That way they'd see no point in striving to do good, and would settle for the easy way out. As it is, some of them seem to think that the road to heaven is hell anyhow! Indeed, some of them are so stupid that they think the road to hell is heaven ! More prolonged applause – and still no approval from Satan! No, no. They would never buy that either. Anyone who knows anything about human nature would never accept that that could work. Human nature is such that, even when today is a mess, they hope that tomorrow will bring an improvement. There is a resilience in people that always holds out something better in the future. No, I'm afraid you'll have to come up with a better plan than that one. Another long pause. Finally, a devil comes to the front, and says: Supposing we go up and tell them that there is a hell, and there is a heaven – but you have plenty of time, and there's no hurry! Satan reached out a hand of congratulations and approval. That's it! he said. That's the plan that will fool them. Go up and convince them of that, and we're really back in business!

Have you heard that whisper lately?

Commitment

At the beginning of John's gospel, the whole thing seems easy and exciting. Jesus turns water into wine, multiplies loaves and fishes, allows Nicodemus avoid social embarrassment by sneaking along to him in the dark, treats the woman at the well with such gentle firmness that she ran off to bring her friends, and he even gives the man at the pool a choice: 'Do you want to be healed?'

In chapter six, however, he really slams them! Unless, unless, unless … you cannot be my disciples. They froze in their tracks. This man is looking for a commitment! This is a hard saying and who can take it? 'Many of his disciples turned away and deserted him' (Jn 6:60-66).

Jesus didn't back off. He didn't soften the demand: in fact he repeated his demand with greater emphasis. They were free to walk away and he wouldn't stop them. They had made a decision. He still may have had some doubts about those who remained – they may not have made any decision, one way or another. So he turned and challenged them: 'Will you also go away?' (Jn 6:67). He wanted to know, he needed to know. Once he got them over that hump he could deepen and quicken the challenge, all the way to Calvary.

I don't think our main concern in the Church should be for those who drop off. We should have an ever-growing concern for those who stay. They are the ones who need the on-going challenge, because some of them may not really have made any decision.

A group of Christians in Russia were praying together in a room, when the door was suddenly broken down by the boot of a soldier, who stood in front of them with a sub-machine gun, and said, 'Any of you who doesn't really believe in Jesus, and what he says, get out now while you have a chance!' One by one different people made their way to the door. A small group remained where they were. They had made their commitment, and were staying, no matter what the consequences. The soldier closed the door, returned to the front of the group, and smiled, as he said, 'Actually, I believe in Jesus too, and we're better off without those!'

There is an urgency about today's world that must be obvious to the most casual observers. Anwar Sadat, the late President of Egypt, said just one week before he was assassinated, that the tragedy about today's world is that the Third World War has already begun, and few people seem to realise it. Some people think that the big bomb will mark the beginning of the Third World War. No, the big bomb will mark the end of it. The war has already begun. There is not a country on this earth that is not embroiled in some kind of struggle against the forces of evil. Just because I myself may not be personally involved in promoting that evil, does not mean that I am on the side of the good. Love is not just the absence of hatred, nor is peace the absence of war. If I am not clearly seen as decidedly on the side of the good, and part of the solution of today's evil, then I must surely be part of the problem. Once again, I state, there is no in-between.

Once a very poor man heard that 'the King of Kings' was coming to a particular village. Not sure what this was all about, but hoping it might present an opportunity to gain some favour, the poor man set off to meet him. He awaited his turn, while his mind was busy listing off all items he would ask for, if the opportunity arose. Finally it was his turn to be presented to the King of Kings. Before he got a word out of his mouth, the King of Kings said: 'And you, what do you have for me?' 'Me? I have nothing to give you.' 'But you must have,' said the King of Kings, 'Everyone has something to share.' 'I have nothing; I have nothing to share,' insisted the poor man. 'You must have; surely you have something to give.' The poor man was really taken aback, and then he took a piece of cloth from his pocket in which he kept some grains of wheat for chewing as he came along the road. He gave one of the grains to the King of Kings, who thanked him, and then turned around and walked away! The poor man was furious, and he walked out the door and down the road, muttering to himself. Not only did he not get anything, but he even had to share some of what he had! After walking for a mile or two, he opened the cloth to get some grains to chew, and there, in the midst of the grains of wheat, was one grain of gold! Suddenly it dawned on him: 'What a fool I've been,' he thought, 'Why didn't I give it all away!' In life, anything I hold onto for myself will die when I die, and anything I share with another will take on an eternal value. 'Every man is a fool who gets rich on earth but not in heaven' (Lk 12:21).

I grew up in a Church that was one large conglomerate block, where 'we all did everything', as it were. In my part of the country, everybody was seen to go to church, and there was some sort of social or parochial momentum that ensured this kind of uniformity. This is no longer the case, and it is not necessarily bad. We can have uniformity and yet not have unity. People can do all the right things for all the wrong reasons. We could well be sacramentalising people who were never evangelised. If the house is built on sand, it must surely come tumbling down (Lk 6:49). Indeed, from the beginning, Jesus' call was always made to the individual. He called them one by one, and then he sent them out two by two. The personal response of each individual, the commitment that was the free and deliberate choice of the person, was the material with which he would then build his Church. There seems to be a return to that individual commitment. It seems that the Church I grew up in is now becoming a much healthier and more authentic reality, comprising smaller groups of much more committed people.

Perhaps I could illustrate how I see the transition by using a simple story. It is a story about a chicken and a pig that were out for a walk one day. The pig was not too bright and tended to repeat what he heard. 'Do you know those people down in that farm-house?' the chicken asked. 'Yes, indeed I do,' replied the pig. 'They are very good people,' remarked the chicken. 'Yes, indeed,' said the pig, 'they are very good people.' 'Do you know what I was thinking?' 'What were you thinking?' 'They are very good to us.' 'They are indeed,' said the pig. 'They are very good to us.' 'I was thinking we should do something for them.' 'A very good idea. And what did you have in mind?' 'I was thinking we should give them something.' 'A splendid idea,' said the pig, 'I agree we should give them something. What did you have in mind?' 'I was thinking,' said the chicken, 'that we should give them bacon and eggs.' The pig stopped in his tracks. 'No way,' he said. 'For you that's only a little inconvenience, but for me it's a total commitment!'

The days of the little inconvenience are over; nothing less than a total commitment is of any use in today's world.

Church

As I wrote the title of this chapter I was momentarily tempted to go on and write at length on what Church is not. Perhaps that reveals a little of my own personal experience of Church over the years. I want to say what Church is not, but I know it would be so much more helpful if I stated simply and clearly what I believe Church to *be*. Church is people, whether those people are in a building, out in a field, or scattered over a thousand mile radius. Church is people who are connected to, and with, each other by the person and message of Jesus. Every gathering or family of people have a certain spirit, be it good or bad. Church is a gathering of people who share the same Spirit, with a capital 'S'.

The Holy Spirit descended on Mary, and Jesus was formed within her. The Spirit within her was actually using her body, her blood, her human organs, to form a body for Jesus. When the same Spirit descended once more, this time on Mary and the apostles at Pentecost, he made use of their bodies, their hands and feet, their whole beings, to form the Body of Jesus once again. We call that Body the Church. It is made up of people who are connected, held together by the Holy Spirit.

A body is made up of parts. It is essential that the parts be different, or we may end up with a body that is all hands, all feet, or all heads! It is also essential that each part recognises that the other parts must be different, and that each has a special, particular, and unique role. Our bodies have many parts, but the many parts make up one body when they are all put together. So it is with the Body of Christ (1 Cor 12:12). 'We are all parts of one Body, we have the same Spirit ...' (Eph 4:4). I have often thought of people who annoy me, of people I find difficult to accept, and get along with, and have tried to discover the real reason for my problem with them. It's hardly too simplistic to say that the main problem is that they are different from me! They all keep doing things I wouldn't do! If I follow through on that thinking, of course, I may have to accept that they are different because God created them so! And the final and logical step of such a process of thinking would be to concede that the reason why God did things that way, was that he considered that one of me was enough!

We have established that the Church is people. The Church is a body, with people as members of that body. The Church is the Body of Christ. Jesus said he would come back. He came back in his Spirit and he lives in his Church. It is essential that we hold that reality, and not confuse Church with buildings, institutions, with a set of rules pinned to a notice board like a Boy Scouts' Den! The Church is people, and all the rules are in the gospel of Jesus Christ. A certain pastor thought his congregation needed a little shock therapy, so he announced that the Church was dead, and the following Sunday they should have a funeral. They were all invited. They turned up in great numbers, out of curiosity! They were surprised to see a large coffin in the sanctuary, and they were invited to file past the coffin, which was open, to view the remains. To their surprise, there was actually nothing in the coffin, but the base of the coffin was a mirror, and, as each one looked in, they found themselves looking at their own reflection! They got the message.

The Holy Spirit is never given to the individual; he is given to the Body. Only when I am a committed member, firmly attached to the Body, and playing my part in the functioning of that Body, can I expect to receive the Holy Spirit into my life. Someone once compared the Church to the FA Cup Final in Wembley, where 100,000 people, badly in need of a bit of exercise, are sitting down criticising twenty two players, badly in need of a rest! What is really needed is to get the spectators down out of the stands, and get them involved in the action. You just cannot tell me what's wrong with the Church, unless you agree that this means what's wrong with us. In the Church, as in today's world, if we are not part of the solution, we are probably part of the problem.

A better and clearer concept of Church is obtained, I think, if we temporarily substitute the word *community* for *Church*. How did Jesus see Church? He saw it as a body of believers who were one in mind and heart, who showed that they belonged to him by their love for each other (Jn 13:35), and, by the evidence and witness of their unity, they would show to the whole world that the Father sent Jesus (Jn 17:21). He saw the breaking of the bread and the drinking from the same cup as a beautiful and public sign of a commitment to unity and love.

As a Roman Catholic I often wonder if we don't have far too many Masses in this country. A Mass that is not the authentic celebration of community that Jesus intended it to be, is one Mass too many. Let us approach community (Church) from another angle. Suppose I took a large mirror off the wall, dropped it on the ground, and shattered it. Now I pick up each piece and hand one each to a large group of assembled people. Each person has received a different piece of the mirror – some quite small, others larger, some with jagged edges, others with fancy shapes – all different. Now putting that mirror back together again is an example of community-building. Each person reflects Christ in a slightly different way, and it is only when we have put all of the pieces together that we can hope, as a community, to reflect the face of Christ. Putting the pieces together, forming the Body of Christ, and reflecting his face to those who pass by – that is central to the community, to Church.

Let us examine our conscience about what we think Church is, and what we experience it to be. Like the pastor referred to in an earlier paragraph, maybe we, too, should have a funeral. I am not at all pessimistic about the Church. The Church that Jesus founded has his guarantee that the gates of hell will not prevail against it, and it is entrusted with the keys of the kingdom of heaven (Mt 16:18-19). Jesus guarantees to be with his Church always, even to the end of the world (Mt 28:20). The question we must keep asking, however, is, 'Can we, in conscience, honestly believe that what we call Church is, in reality, the Church of Jesus Christ?'

I often think of the advice given by Gamaliel to his fellow council members regarding their approach to dealing with the Church of the apostles: 'If what they do and teach is merely of their own, it will soon be overthrown. But if it is of God, you will not be able to stop them' (Acts 5:38-39). If we are to have any hopes for survival in today's world, surely then it must be by doing all we can to ensure that what we do and say is really from God, is truly according to the mind of Christ.

As I said in an earlier chapter, when Jesus sent his Spirit, he asked, and expected us to provide the Body. Unless that Body is seen to be united in love through the working of the Holy Spirit, it can lose all credibility. People today are still climbing the mountainside looking for Jesus (Jn 6:5). If the people of today come to our Church and do not find Jesus there, then we can rightly be dismissed as being irrelevant. The witness value of the Church is crucial, and that is why I want to deal with that in the next chapter.

Christian Witness

The cross is more than just a Christian symbol, but a symbol it definitely is. There is a direct connection between the vertical and the horizontal, between what comes from God to me, and what goes from me to others. Unless forgiveness goes from me to others, it doesn't come from God. God doesn't want to hear me say to him, 'I love you, I thank you, I praise you, I'm sorry,' unless others in my life hear it first. Whenever I approach God, I must always experience the challenge of how I relate to those around me. 'If you bring your gift to the altar and there you remember that your brother has something against you, leave your gift before the altar, go and be reconciled to your brother, and then come and offer your gift.' No room for any doubts or quibbling there!

Jesus lays great stress on the evidence or *witness* of Christian living. 'Let your light shine before men that they may see your good works' (Mt 5:16). 'By this shall all men know that you are my disciples, if you love one another' (Jn 13:35). 'May they be one, as we are one, Father, so that the world may know that you sent me' (Jn 17:23).

Jesus was asked by the disciples of John the Baptist, 'Are you the one who is to come, or shall we look for another?' and Jesus simply asked them to look around and see for themselves. All the signs, all the witness was there. Just go back and tell John what you have seen and heard.

I often imagine what might happen if a man from Mars were to land in our Churches some Sunday morning, and ask us if we were true followers of Jesus. Would he have to look elsewhere? Would we have enough evidence to convince him? The question was once asked, 'If we were arrested, brought to the nearest police station, and charged with being Christians, how many of us would get off scot-free for lack of evidence?'

A Christian is not someone who is striving to get to heaven, but he is doing what he can to get heaven down here. It is often so much more difficult to get heaven into people, than to get people into heaven! A Christian is in the business of attracting, not promoting.

Jesus is the way – the early Christians were known as followers of the way. In other words, they knew where they were going! The following epitaph appears on an old tombstone in an English country churchyard:

Dear stranger, pause as you pass by:
As you are now, so once was I.
As I am now, so you shall be,
– So prepare yourself to follow me.

To which some wit added with a piece of chalk:
To follow you I'm quite content,
But how do I know which way you went?

A Christian is someone who is saved, and who looks saved! If I'm on my way to heaven, then I should look like someone on his way to heaven! Jesus asks, 'Why be like the pagans … why be like the heathen ?' (Mt 6:31), when he reproves us about the anxieties and lack of faith in our lives.

Christianity has never actually failed – it just hasn't been tried too often! I myself have experienced Christianity being truly lived on a few occasions, and in a few places, and it was an extraordinary experience. I felt I could bring the greatest cynic, the most vociferous agnostic, or the most hardened sinner into that environment, and expect hearts to be touched and melted. There is no denying the extraordinary witness and power of real love.

In a way I feel that Christianity is on trial in today's world. Let me put it this way, by using figures from a seminar on evangelisation in Switzerland a few years ago. Imagine there are only 100 people on this earth, all in the one village. On today's facts, 67 of them would be poor, while 33 of them would be in various levels of being well-off. 93 of them would have to watch while 7 of them spend half the money, have half the bath tubs, and eat one third of the food – while those 7 would have ten times as many doctors looking after them as the other 93 put together. That is not the real problem though, from our point of view. The real problem is when the 7 have the nerve and the gall to attempt to evangelise the 93! They tell them about the beautiful Saviour they have, who talks about sharing, feeding the hungry etc. while the 7 throw out more food than would feed all of the 93! They build bigger and better basilicas and cathedrals for this God of theirs, while the 93 find it increasingly difficult to find a place to live. They transfer monies, and open new and better bank accounts, while the 93 find it becoming more and more difficult to get something to eat. The bottom line must surely be this: If the 7 are so stupid and so blind that they cannot see the frightful contradiction of their situation, then, surely, they cannot expect the 93 to be that stupid, to be that blind!

In the early Church, the company of believers, the followers of the way, were very much a minority among their countrymen, and a real mystery to most of them. They may have seemed 'full of wine' to some, or dangerous subversives to others. One thing could not be denied by the on-lookers, and it drew forth their begrudging admiration, 'See how these Christians love one another.' There is no denying the witness of real love. Any expression of Christianity that does not give clear and positive evidence of real love is a travesty, and a betrayal of the message of the gospel!

As members of the Body of Christ, we have a serious responsibility to make Jesus present again among our people. We do this by our unity and active love. If you come across the Body of Christ without the wounds, then be sure it is a phoney! Our families, our gatherings, our parishes, all have wounded members, and our love is really shown in our dealings with them. There is no denying the evidence of real love, and it is at the heart of Christian witness.

A World of Justice

The biggest sin in today's world is the sin of injustice. One section of the world's population has much more than its rightful share of the world's wealth and food, while the other section is deprived of basic requirements, and is dying of hunger. It is not my intention here to go into the statistics of all this, but to look at the situation of today's world, and see what Christianity should, and must be doing about it. According to Mt 25, the final judgement will not be based on whether we were moved by private spiritual experiences. No, the measure of final judgement is scandalously materialistic. It has to do with food, drink, clothing, and being a friend to the imprisoned and to the oppressed. And the glaring evidence of today's world is that, two thousand years after Jesus spelt out his message and his formula for a better world, there are still endless thousands who are hungry, thirsty, naked, strangers, in prison, and grievously oppressed.

A few years ago I was speaking to a person who is

working with lepers in Calcutta. One of the first sights he saw there when he arrived was the vast homeless hopeless multitudes, just sitting on the side-walks: no social security of any kind, and the hand held out, in some cases, had no fingers. Among this mass of humanity, he spotted a little old man sitting in the gutter, and there were two rats eating his foot. Because he had leprosy he couldn't feel anything, and because he was blind he couldn't see anything – and nobody, but nobody paid the slightest attention to what was happening. My friend's initial reaction was one of anger at the rest of the world. He experienced what George Washington expressed when he cried out, 'Does anybody out there see what I see? Does anybody out there care? Does anybody out there hear me? Is there anybody out there?' When I asked my friend what was the most difficult thing about working with lepers in Calcutta, his answer jolted me. He is a gentle soul, he is not a cynic, and yet his reply was, 'The most difficult thing about working with lepers here in Calcutta, is to have to return to any of the countries in the West, and hear the concerns and worries of the Christian Church, and the questions that preoccupy their church-going population: "Should we, or should we not, have Masses on Saturday evenings? Should guitars and such like be allowed in our Churches? Should we, or should we not, have more positive ongoing dialogue with other Christian Churches?" Their concerns are so far removed from the real problems of today's world, that one would wonder if we are reading from the same gospel at all!'

I have chosen to call this book *It's really very simple*, because that is how I see the gospel. I have kept this chapter to the end for several reasons. The main reason, to be honest about it, is that I myself am only now beginning to come to grips with, and to make some positive response, to the cries of the poor and the oppressed in our world. Another reason is that I need to clarify for myself, again and again, just what gospel I'm talking about, when I say that it's very simple. I have to keep reminding myself that Jesus came to preach good news to the poor, to feed the hungry, to set prisoners free. He sends us to do the same in his name. There is only one gospel, the good news of Jesus. Like a schoolboy writing an essay, we have to continually lift our eyes off the page and look again at the title – and make sure that's what we are writing about. Jesus came to comfort the afflicted, but he also came to afflict the comfortable.

The concept of mission in the Church seems to be undergoing radical changes. We no longer send missioners to Africa or to India to convert anyone, and to get them to accept certain doctrines. Nowadays, it seems that the missioner can very well help the people in their struggle against injustice and oppression, even if this means helping the Hindu to become a better Hindu, or the Muslim to become a better Muslim. In doing this, the missioner will become a better Christian. It is the missioner himself who will be converted with this approach. This makes it possible for the poor we work with to evangelise us. I really believe that the poor of the world will evangelise the rest of us if we let them.

Jesus compares his relationship with us to that of a shepherd and his sheep (Jn 10:1-10). The parable is clear and simple. It is the day of judgement. The king is on his throne, and he separates the sheep from the goats; the sheep on his right go to eternal life, the goats on his left go to eternal damnation. The element of surprise in the parable is that both the sheep and the goats are utterly astonished to find the degree to which Jesus has identified himself with the poor, the needy, the oppressed. Those on his right have, of course, been feeding the hungry, putting clothes on the poor, and taking care of the sick, but they are completely surprised to hear Jesus say that when they were doing that they were ministering to him. Those on the left are even more surprised to hear Jesus identify himself so completely with the poor and the oppressed. They are shocked: if they had known that Jesus was in need, of course they would have done anything for him.

But they hadn't ministered to all those poor, help-less, and sick people, because they were too busy being religious, and pious, and worrying about the letter of the law. What a surprise it was to learn that, in not ministering to them, they had rejected Jesus! Both groups are equally shocked to discover that their eternal destiny is being determined by just a few questions. There are no questions about how often they went to church, what theology they had learned, or how successful they had been in life. These questions are not raised. The questions that determine their destiny are: Did you feed the hungry? Did you take care of the sick? Did you visit those who are in prison or in special need?

There are two statements of Jesus in the gospels that must always and ever be kept to the fore and meditated and acted on: 'Whatever you did to the least of these, that's what you did unto me' (Mt 25 :40). The second statement is: 'I am going away, and the world won't see me anymore – but you will, because you know me' (Jn 14:19). The world has never seen Jesus in the poor, the down-trod-den, or the oppressed, or, indeed, the unborn. The acid test of our knowing him, however, is that we will see him in all of these. 'You will, because you know me.' G. G. Studdert Kennedy (1884-1929) wrote:

When Jesus came to Golgotha they hanged him
on a tree,
They drove great nails through hands and feet
and made a Calvary,
They crowned him with a crown of thorns, red
were his wounds and deep,
For those were crude and cruel days, and human
flesh was cheap.
When Jesus came to Birmingham they simply
passed him by.
They never hurt a hair of him, they only let him
die:
For men had grown more tender, and they would
not give him pain:
They only just passed down the street, and left
him in the rain.

Still Jesus cried, forgive them, for they know not
what they do,
And still it rained a wintry rain that drenched him
through and through,
The crowds went home and left the streets with-
out a soul to see,
And Jesus crouched against a wall, and cried for
Calvary.

The abiding problem in Christianity is that
Christians want to be committed to Christ, without
being committed to Christ's brothers and sisters.

But Christ has closed that option. He has so arranged it that he is not to be found, or served, apart from his brothers or sisters. Service to our King is social action. It may involve great social movements or political causes, or it may be for most of us the day-by-day work of ministering in love to just a few who need our help. In any case, it is social.

Once a village blacksmith had a vision. An angel came to tell him that God was calling him home to the fullness of the Kingdom. I thank God for thinking of me, replied the blacksmith, but as you know, the season for sowing the crops is beginning and, as I am the only blacksmith in these parts, who will help these poor people when a horse needs to be shod, or a plough needs to be fixed? I don't wish to appear ungrateful, but do you think I could put off taking my place in the kingdom until I have finished? I'll see what can be done, said the angel, as he vanished. The angel returned a year or two later with the same message. This time, however, a farmer was seriously ill, and the blacksmith was trying to save his crop for him, so that his family wouldn't suffer. The angel was sent back to see what could be done. This happened again and again, and on each occasion the blacksmith just spread his hands in a gesture of resignation and compassion, and drew the angel's attention to where the suffering was, and where his help was needed. Eventually, the blacksmith felt very old and tired, and he prayed, Lord, if you would like to send your angel again, I think I'd be happy to see him. The angel appeared. If you still want to take me, said the blacksmith, I am ready to take up my abode in the Lord's kingdom. The angel looked at the blacksmith in surprise and said, where do you think you've been all these years?

I am very much aware that I can only hope to touch on the whole area of the cry of the poor and the oppressed in today's world. I won't dare suggest any solutions. All I hope to do is to awaken both my conscience, and that of the reader, to the reality that exists. When I asked my friend from Calcutta if he might suggest something we could do to help in such a situation, his reply was immediate and brief. Stay at home, and start at home. In *Cry the Beloved Country*, Alan Paton writes, 'Do not look for me just in the sanctuaries, or in the precise words of theologians, or in the calm of the country-side: Look for me in the place where men are struggling for their very survival as human beings.' When I am ready, when I am willing, when I appreciate the great privilege of ministering to Jesus in his poor, then I will find his poor.